Jackie
Hope you get blessed
& enjoy.
JoAnn Duncan

THE ESSENTIAL WORD

JO DUNCAN

WestBow Press
A Division of Thomas Nelson
& Zondervan

Copyright © 2014 Jo Duncan.

All rights reserved. No part of this book may be used or reproduced by any means, graphic, electronic, or mechanical, including photocopying, recording, taping or by any information storage retrieval system without the written permission of the publisher except in the case of brief quotations embodied in critical articles and reviews.

WestBow Press books may be ordered through booksellers or by contacting:

WestBow Press
A Division of Thomas Nelson & Zondervan
1663 Liberty Drive
Bloomington, IN 47403
www.westbowpress.com
1 (866) 928-1240

Because of the dynamic nature of the Internet, any web addresses or links contained in this book may have changed since publication and may no longer be valid. The views expressed in this work are solely those of the author and do not necessarily reflect the views of the publisher, and the publisher hereby disclaims any responsibility for them.

Any people depicted in stock imagery provided by Thinkstock are models, and such images are being used for illustrative purposes only. Certain stock imagery © Thinkstock.

ISBN: 978-1-4908-4756-6 (sc)
ISBN: 978-1-4908-4757-3 (e)

Library of Congress Control Number: 2014914051

Printed in the United States of America.

WestBow Press rev. date: 9/30/2014

PREFACE

When I first started reading the 2 chapters Old Testament, 2 chapters New Testament, 5 chapters Psalms and 1 chapter Proverbs daily, a dear friend, Barbara joined me and her excitement and encouragement kept me going. We talked every day sharing the things we learned.

I rearranged the schedule that we used (2 chapters a day took 374 days to finish the Old Testament).

Some people think the Old Testament is just history or a covenant for some other people, but when Jesus was tempted by the devil, He said, "It is written" and those powerful scriptures were all from Deuteronomy. Paul quoted scripture from the OT constantly.

My favorite translation for in-depth study is: Amplified, and the footnotes are awesome. Reading ease is the New King James, It is more accurate than many of the new translations; and King James for memorizing.

Romans 10:17 "Faith comes by hearing and hearing by the word of God."

Hebrews 5:12-13 "For though by this time you ought to be teachers, you need someone to teach you again the first principles of the oracles of God; and you have come to need milk and not solid food. For everyone who partakes only of milk is unskilled in the word of righteousness, for he is a babe."

New Testament is milk and as a babe you first need a good foundation, and Old Testament is meat.

Because of copyright limits, Scriptures quoted through Day 79 are in New King James and the remainder is New American Standard unless otherwise noted.

Special thanks to Lee Thomas for permission to refer to his excellent book, "Praying Effectively for the Lost" on Day 28.

I hope and pray that this will bless you tremendously.

Jo Duncan

Day 1 Gen 1-2; Mt 1-2; Ps 1-5; Pr 1

I believe the time line was:

Gen 1:1 "In the beginning God created the heavens and the earth."

Rev 12:7-9 "And war broke out in heaven: Michael and his angels fought with the dragon; and the dragon and his angels fought, but they did not prevail, nor was there a place found for them in heaven any longer. So the great dragon was cast out, that serpent of old, called the Devil and Satan."

Gen 1:2 "The earth was without form and void (the meaning of void and darkness are from Strong's Concordance. Void is 922- empty: a vacuity, a ruin); and darkness (2822-darkness; misery, destruction, death, ignorance, sorrow, wickedness) was on the face of the deep."

Ezek 28:17 & Is 14:12 There was life on earth before the devil was cast down, it was destroyed in his rage. The evil Satan was certainly present in the Garden with Adam. When God said "Let there be light," it was a battle cry that shook the universe because that light was Jesus! The light on the first day had to be Jesus because the sun, stars, seasons, days and years were created on the fourth day.

John 1:1-3 "In the beginning was the Word and the Word was with God, and the Word was God. He was in the beginning with God. All things were made through Him, and without Him nothing was made that was made."

Since God skips a lot of detail, I wonder if the dinosaurs were killed when Satan fell to earth instead of in Noah's flood, as some assume.

The Essential Word 1

Some scientists believe they were destroyed when a great comet hit the earth, just a thought, (see Luke 10:18).

Day 2 Gen 3-4; Mt 3-4; Ps 6-10; Pr 2

Gen 3:15 "And I will put enmity between you and the woman, and between your seed and her Seed; he shall bruise your head, and you shall bruise His heel." This is the first prophecy of the coming of Jesus.

This is probably why so many travailing intercessors are women (travail in birth began here.) Men can be very powerful in prayer of course, but how many people will say they had a mother or grandmother who prayed for them and would not let go of them until they came back to the faith that was taught to them as a child. Woman can make up for physical weakness with great tenacity.

Gen 3:21 Sin can't be covered with fig leaves. Those who think they earn salvation through works or being good enough are following an empty religion for only the Blood of Jesus will take away sin. God performed the first animal sacrifice and made clothing to cover their nakedness.

Gen 4:3 Cain's offering was not accepted and Abel's was because the "Law" was already in effect and he had to have a sin offering (blood) to cover his sin before he could approach God with a thank offering.

In Gen 7:2 Noah is instructed to take 2 unclean and 7 clean animals on the ark. The clean animals were needed for food and sacrificing to the Lord, so the Law is obviously in effect at that time.

Day 3 Gen 5-6; Mt 5-6; Ps 11-15; Pr 3

Forgive---Forgive---Forgive---Forgive---Forgive

Mt 6:12&14 "And forgive us our debts, as we forgive our debtors. For if you forgive men their trespasses, your heavenly father will also forgive you. But if you do not forgive men their trespasses, neither will your heavenly father forgive your trespasses.

Luke 6:37, 38 "Judge not, and you shall not be judged, condemn not and you will not be condemned….Give and it will be given to you, good measure, pressed down, shaken together and running over will be put into your bosom, for with the same measure that you use, it will be measured back to you…."

I've often heard this verse quoted to mean good things will be given to me. BUT, I sure don't want judgment and condemnation measured back to me.

Forgiveness is the most overlooked weapon in our arsenal toward the salvation of someone we are praying for and victory in our own life.

Mt 16:19 "And I will give you the keys of the kingdom of heaven, and whatever you bind on earth will be bound in heaven, and whatever you loose on earth will be loosed in heaven."

He has given us awesome responsibility! How will you feel if standing before the judgment seat, a friend of yours or someone who had hurt you stands condemned and the Father turns and asks, "Who had the key?"

Day 4 Gen 7-8; Mt 7-8; Ps 16-20; Pr 4

Mt 7:11 "If you then, evil as you are, know how to give good and advantageous gifts to your children, how much more will your Father Who is in heaven (perfect as He is) give good and advantageous things to those who keep on asking Him!" (Amplified Bible)

What better gift can your Father give than the salvation of someone you have travailed for? Women travail to give birth and sometimes the pain is short and sometimes it takes many hours. Can we expect to give birth in the spirit in a few minutes? Pray until you feel the release. What greater joy can you receive than from a loved one being saved? What if the one who is saved has been your enemy? When you obey and pray for that person you do not like, you will find ill will melting away, to be replaced by a sincere wish for them to be blessed.

Mt 5:44 "But I say to you, love your enemies, bless those who curse you, do good to those who hate you, and pray for those who spitefully use you."

The salvation of that one will be a great joy also and possibly make them a close and dear friend.

Day 5 Gen 9-10; Mt 9-10; Ps 21-25; Pr 5

Mt 10:1 & 8 The disciples were given power over unclean spirits, to cast them out, and to heal all kinds of sickness and all kinds of diseases. Jesus said, go, "Heal the sick, cleanse the lepers, raise the dead, cast out demons. Freely you have received, freely give."

Luke 10:1 & 17-19 The Lord sent out seventy more. "Then the seventy returned with joy, saying, Lord, even the demons are subject to us in Your name. And He said to them, 'I saw Satan fall like lightning from heaven. Behold, I give you the authority to trample on serpents and scorpions, and over all the power of the enemy, and nothing shall by any means hurt you."

This is before Jesus was sacrificed and the Holy Spirit sent to us. We don't begin to tap in to a tenth of the power and authority that is available to us.

Day 6 Gen 11-12; Mt 11-12; Ps 26-30; Pr 6

Gen 11:6 "And the Lord said, 'Indeed the people are one and they all have one language, and this is what they began to do; now nothing that they propose to do will be withheld from them."

But Christians should have one purpose and the language of the redeemed in common. So why do we feel so helpless? Because we do not have the power of unity we are supposed to have.

Ps 1:2 Do we meditate on the Law of the Lord day and night?

The Essential Word

II Cor 10:4 Do we understand that the weapons of our warfare are mighty to pull down the strongholds of the devil?

I Th 5:17 Do we pray without ceasing?

I Tim 2:8 Do we pray everywhere lifting up holy hands, without wrath and doubting?

James 1:22 It is time to become doers of the word and not hearers only, deceiving ourselves.

Mt 18:19 "Again I say to you that if two of you agree on earth concerning anything that they ask, it will be done for them by My Father in heaven."

It is time to seek unity and gain strength for the business of the Lord. The Lords business is not adding numbers in our local Church, but adding souls in His Kingdom.

Day 7 Gen 13-14; Mt 13-14; Ps 31-35; Pr 7

Mt 13:37-43 Seed is sown in the world. The righteous are sown by the Lord and the evil are sown by the devil. They grow together until the end of the age. The evil are gathered and thrown into the fire, then the righteous are gathered into God's kingdom.

Mt 13:47-50 Again the kingdom of heaven is like a dragnet and at the end of the age all are pulled in together and the righteous and evil are separated.

Mt 25:31-34 "When the Son of Man comes in His glory and all the holy angels with Him, then He will sit on the throne of His glory. All the nations will be gathered before Him, and He will separate them one from another, as a shepherd divides his sheep from the goats."

There has been a lot of speculation about the end of time. Some think that Christians will be taken out of the world before the end, but these scriptures do not show that. The best we can do is be prepared for the worst and pray that the Lord will give us strength for whatever comes to us.

Day 8 Gen 15-16; Mt 15-16; Ps 36-40; Pr 8

Gen 15: 18-21 A covenant is made between God and the descendants of Abraham. Enemies would be forced out of the land of their inheritance.

Gal 3:29 "And if you are Christ's, then you are Abraham's seed, and heirs according to the promise" These enemies apply to us also, enemies we must fight inch by inch and yard by yard.

These are definitions of the enemy's names from Strong's Exhaustive Concordance:

Kenites---to strike a musical note, i.e. chant or wail (at a funeral)--Lament, mourning woman.

Kenezzites---to hunt, hunter

Kadmonites---ancient, i.e. aboriginal,--they that went before

Hittites---to prostrate, hence to breakdown, either (lit) by violence or (fig) by confusion and fear, abolish, affright, be (make) afraid, amaze, beat down, discourage, (cause to) dismay, go down, scare, terrify.

The Essential Word IIII 7

Perizzites---an open country--unwalled town, unwalled village; to separate

Raphaim---in the sense of invigorating, a giant:--slacken, abate, cease, consume, be faint, wax feeble, forsake, idle slothful, weak, weaken

Amorites---in the sense of publicity, i.e. prominence; thus a mountaineer:--boast self, challenge, demand, determine.

Canaanites---humiliated,--to bend the knee; hence to humiliate, vanquish;--bring down (low) into subjection, under, humble, subdue

Girgashites---dwellers on clay soil (from Cruden's Concordance, no definition in Strong's) unfruitful, barren.

Jebusites---trodden, i.e. threshing place--to trample (lit or fig) loath, tread (down under foot); be polluted.

These are traits that don't belong to Christians;--mournful, being a victim, fear, pride, fruitless, beaten down.

Our goal is joy, security, humility, bearing the fruit of the Spirit and being victorious.

Day 9 Gen 17-18; Mt 17-18; Ps 41-45; Pr 9

Gen 17:11 "and you shall be circumcised in the flesh of your foreskins, and it shall be a sign of the covenant between Me and you."

De 30:6 "And the Lord your God will circumcise your heart and the heart of your descendants, to love the Lord your God with all your heart and with all your soul that you may live."

Jer 4:4 "Circumcise yourselves to the Lord, and take away the foreskins of your hearts…."

Col 2:11-12 "In Him also you were circumcised with a circumcision not made with hands, but in a (spiritual) circumcision (performed by) Christ by stripping off the body of the flesh (the whole corrupt, carnal nature with its passions and lusts). Thus you were circumcised when you were buried with Him in (your) baptism, in which you were also raised with Him to a new Life through your faith in the working of God (as displayed) when He raised Him up from the dead." (Amplified Bible)

Both baptism and circumcision are symbolic of the covenant God seeks with us when we yield our will to Him.

Day 10 Gen 19-20; Mt 19-20; Ps 46-50; Pr 10

Gen 12:13-15 You would think a man hearing the voice of God and speaking directly to Him, would not allow his wife to be taken into a harem for fear of his life. Abraham seemed to be more concerned for Lot. He didn't hesitate to ask for Lot to be rescued. Lots wife loved the city of Sodom and her life there so she looked back and was turned into a pillar of salt.

Luke 9: 62 But Jesus said to him, "No one having put his hand to the plow, and looking back, is fit for the kingdom of God."

We have things in our life that we love and when we come to Jesus we have a lot of baggage to get rid of. I love to read and when I became serious about being a Christian, I packed up my collection (about 300) novels and got them out of my home. After some time passed I went back to reading and acquired several hundred more books again. I had to face my problem and truly understand what I was doing.

I'm not saying that reading is a sin, but I can't allow it to consume all my spare time. I see people watching hours of football, and wonder if they realize how much time it takes from their life, of course I hate football so I would naturally think it is a waste of time. Today we are faced with entertainment and distraction everywhere. James, the brother of Jesus is reputed to have had "camel's knees" from spending so much time in prayer. Do we have people like that today?

Day 11 Gen 21-22; Mt 21-22; Ps 51-55; Pr 11

Gal 4:28-31 "Now we, brethren, as Isaac was, are children of promise. But, as he who was born according to the flesh then persecuted him who was born according to the Spirit, even so it is now, Nevertheless what does the Scripture say? "Cast out the bondwoman and her son, for the son of the bondwoman shall not be heir with the son of the free-woman." So then, we are not children of the bondwoman but of the free."

Abraham loved both of his sons. But there was jealousy in Ishmael, and Abraham had to send him away.

The spirit of jealousy and hatred that began with Ishmael toward Isaac is still in the descendants of Ishmael today. How else can the hatred be explained for Israel, a people who hunger for peace? How else do you explain the continued survival of a people surrounded by hostile forces? Through the purges of the past there has always remained a remnant to survive and grow again. We Christians are hated also because we are bound by covenant and are linked in the Spirit to Israel. The hatred comes from the god of this world, the father of all hatred.

John 15:18 "If the world hates you, you know that it hated Me before it hated you."

Day 12 Gen 23-24; Mt 23-24; Ps 56-60; Pr 12

Ps 56..A Michtam (poem) of David when the Philistines captured him in Gath (I Sam 21: 10-15)

I Sam 13:14 God said David was a man after His own heart. Whatever David went through he was singing songs of praise to the Lord. What do we do in response to the trials of life? We probably complain, cry, fall into depression and hopefully before long remember that we are not alone. David starts with "Have mercy" and then states his trust and confidence. David had learned to trust the Lord with every moment of his life.

Ps 23:4 "Yea, though I walk through the valley of the shadow of death, I will fear no evil; for You are with me Your rod and Your staff, they comfort me."

The rod is for correction and the staff is for guidance. We can have total confidence in the Father who works for our good always. When I prayed for two of my children and finally abandoned them into the hands of God, a seeming disaster happened. After spending Sunday afternoon crying and wringing my hands, I got up Monday morning, raised my hands up toward the ceiling and yelled "No!, I believe God and I believe Jeremiah 29:11 and Romans 8:28 and this is going to be a good thing." Instantly peace came on me and I never totally lost sight of the working of God through what would otherwise have been a hideous ordeal.

Jeremiah 29:11 "For I know the thoughts and plans that I have for you, says the Lord, thoughts and plans for welfare and peace and not of evil, to give you hope in your final outcome." (Amplified Bible)

Romans 8:28 "And we know that all things work together for good to those who love God, to those who are the called according to His purpose"

There is no peace without trust.

Day 13 Gen 25-26; Mt 25-26; Ps 61-65; Pr 13

Gen 26:3-4 "Dwell in this land, and I will be with you and bless you; for to you and your descendants I give all these lands, and I will perform the oath which I swore to Abraham your father. And I will make your descendants multiply as the stars of heaven; I will give to your descendants all these lands; and in your seed all the nations of the earth shall be blessed;"

The land was a physical land and yet the promises come to our generation of a spiritual land; His Rest.

Ps 143:10 "Teach me to do Your will, for You are my God; Your Spirit is good. Lead me in the land of uprightness."

Heb 3: 7-11 & Ps 95:11 "Therefore, as the Holy Spirit says: Today, if you will hear His voice, Do not harden your hearts as in the rebellion, In the day of trial in the wilderness, Where your fathers tested Me, tried Me, And saw My works forty years. Therefore I was angry with that generation, and said, "They always go astray in their heart, and they have not known My ways." So I swore in My wrath, they shall not enter My Rest."

Day 14 Gen 27-28; Mt 27-28; Ps 66-70; Pr 14

This is some of Jesus' suffering that was foretold in the Old Testament:

Is 50: 5-7 "The Lord has opened My ear; and I was not rebellious, Nor did I turn away. I gave My back to those who struck Me, And My cheeks to those who plucked out the beard; I did not hide My face from shame and spitting. For the Lord will help Me; therefore I will not be disgraced; Therefore I have set My face like flint, and I know I will not be ashamed."

Is 52:14-15 "Just as many were astonished at you; So His visage was marred more than any man, And His form more than the sons of men; so shall He sprinkle many nations."

Ps 22:1-18 "… all My bones are out of joint; …My tongue clings to My jaws …they pierced My hands and My feet; I can count all My bones; …"

Is 53:3-7 "He is despised and rejected by men, A Man of sorrows; Yet we esteemed Him stricken, Smitten by God, and afflicted, But He was wounded for our transgressions, He was bruised for our iniquities; The chastisement for our peace was upon Him, And by His stripes we are healed. All we like sheep have gone astray; we have turned, every one, to his own way; and the Lord has laid on Him the iniquity of us all. He was oppressed and He was afflicted, Yet He opened not His mouth; He was led as a lamb to the slaughter, and as a sheep before its shearers is silent, So He opened not His mouth."

Jesus suffered all the physical pain in silence. The only time He cried out was when the sin of all mankind was laid on Him and His Father turned His face away.

Day 15 Gen 29-30; Mark 1-2; Ps 71-75; Pr 15

Then the Pharisees and scribes asked Him why His disciples did not follow the tradition of the elders, about the washing of hands.

Mark 2:27 "And He said to them, 'The Sabbath was made for man, and not man for the Sabbath." The priests had turned the Law into a set of rules that was so huge there was no way to obey them all.

Acts 15:10 "Now therefore, why do you test God by putting a yoke on the neck of the disciples which neither our fathers nor we were able to bear?" "Woe to you scribes and Pharisees, hypocrites! For you cleanse the outside of the cup and dish, but inside they are full of extortion and self-indulgence." There was nothing from the heart, only empty ritual.

Mark 7:3-5 "For the Pharisees and all the Jews do not eat unless they wash their hands in a special way, holding the tradition of the elders. When they come from the marketplace they do not eat unless they wash. And there are many other things which they have received and hold, like the washing of cups, pitchers, copper vessels, and couches."

The religious leaders had no love for the people; they were only jealous and protective of their power.

Day 16 Gen 31-32; Mark 3-4; Ps 76-80; Pr 16

Gen 27:6-13 Rebekah, who had instigated Jacob stealing the blessing from Esau, never saw her favorite son again. She sent Jacob to her brother Laban and spent the rest of her life with the daughters-in-law that she despised.

Laban was a sneaky, self-seeking man (very similar to Jacob) whose conscience didn't bother him much. Jacob was blessed because of the Lord's promises and not because he deserved it.

Gen 31 After working seven years for Rachel, Laban pulled a switch and gave him Leah. Jacob served another seven years for Rachel. When Jacob was ready to move on, Laban asked him to stay. As Jacob was working another seven years for his share of the herds, Laban kept changing the deal, ten times. What Laban meant for evil, God turned for good, (God just loves to do that) and Jacob had large flocks because God intervened and didn't allow Jacob to be cheated. So, Jacob went away with herds of sheep, goats, camels, cattle and donkeys. He came to Laban with nothing and came back very wealthy.

The Essential Word ▬ 15

Day 17 Gen 33-34; Mark 5-6; Ps 81-85; Pr 17

When Jesus fed thousands of people He was showing them the work of the prophet Elisha.

II K 4:42-44 "...and he said, 'Give it to the people, that they may eat.' But his servant said. 'What? Shall I set this before one hundred men?' He said again 'Give it to the people; that they may eat; for thus says the Lord; 'They shall eat and have some left over.' So he set it before them; and they ate and had some left over."

Mark 6:41-44 "And when He had taken the five loaves and the two fish, He looked up to heaven, blessed and broke the loaves, and gave them to His disciples to set before them; and the two fish He divided among them all. So they all ate and were filled. And they took up twelve baskets full of fragments and of the fish. Now those who had eaten the loaves were about five thousand men."

The people were expecting the Messiah because of the prophecy in Daniel 9:24-26. It was time, the year, the right family, the city He would be born into. And yet this Jesus didn't fit their idea of the Messiah. There were two kinds of prophecy, the servant and the conquering king.

Suffering under Roman rule they were wanting a warrior king. This is one reason the Jews rejected Jesus, which was God's plan. Luke 24:7

Day 18 Gen 35-36; Mark 7-8; Ps 86-90; Pr 18

Pr 18:21 "Death and life are in the power of the tongue, and those who love it will eat its fruit."

Gossip destroys a reputation, and even if it is true, it is wrong to pass it on to the eager ear. Many have suffered from vicious tongues and relationships have been destroyed.

Ps 64:2-4 "Hide me from the secret plots of the wicked, from the rebellion of the workers of iniquity, who sharpen their tongue like a sword, and bend their bows to shoot their arrows---bitter words, that they may shoot in secret at the blameless;"

James 1:26 "If anyone among you thinks he is religious, and does not bridle his tongue but deceives his own heart, this one's religion is useless."

James 3:6 "And the tongue is a fire, a world of iniquity..."

Mt 12:35-36 "A good man out of the good treasure of his heart brings forth good things, and an evil man out the evil treasure brings forth evil things. But I say to you that for every idle word men may speak, they will give account of it in the day of judgment."

We are forgiven through the Blood of Jesus, but it is still important to remember that our words have tremendous power to sooth or stir up, to heal relationships or break them. We may not be thrown into Hell for our words, but we will be answerable for them.

Day 19 Gen 37-38; Mark 9-10; Ps 91-95; Pr 19

Joseph (type of Christ) was the beloved son of his father. His brothers were already jealous because of the favor shown by their father. When he told them about the visions sent to him from God they were moved to hatred. Then the opportunity came to get rid of him. Some wanted to kill him, but Reuben intervened by saying they should throw Joseph in a pit and not bear the curse of innocent blood.

Reuben hoped to release Joseph later and return him to their father. The brothers stripped Joseph of his tunic and threw him into the pit.

A caravan of Ishmaelites came along, so Judah said they should make a profit instead of wasting the opportunity. They sold Joseph for twenty pieces of silver and he went into slavery in Egypt. Joseph rose from slavery to be ruler of Egypt second only to Pharaoh. Joseph was thirty when he began to rule Egypt. When Joseph next faced his brothers they bowed down to the ground before him. When he told his brothers who he was they were afraid, Joseph told them God had planned his going ahead of them for their salvation. The mind set on God will see the big picture.

Day 20 Gen 39-40; Mark 11-12; Ps 96-100; Pr 20

Joseph served loyally in every situation. Potiphar bought Joseph from the Ishmaelites and made him a household slave, and God blessed the household because of Joseph, and he was made overseer. He was unjustly thrown into prison where because of faithfulness he was put in charge of the prisoners.

Pharaoh had dreams that troubled him and no one could interpret them but Joseph. Since none could be found wiser than Joseph, Pharaoh put him in charge of managing the crisis of storing enough food for the seven barren years (a prudent plan for all of us). When the famine came and people had used up all they had stored, they came to Joseph. Finally, Jacob sent his sons to Egypt for grain, but kept Benjamin at home because he was the only son remaining from his beloved Rachel.

Joseph recognized his brothers immediately and when they bowed down to the ground, Joseph remembered his dreams.

Joseph was faithful to the vision given him.

Gal 6:9 "And let us not grow weary while doing good, for in due season we shall reap if we do not lose heart."

Day 21 Gen 41-42; Mark 13-14; Ps 101-105; Pr 21

There is some reason to think that Joseph, serving as the shadow or type of the Christ to come would be in the line of ancestors of Jesus, he was even sold into slavery by his brothers for twenty pieces of silver, Jesus was sold for thirty.

Ps 78:67-68 "Moreover He rejected the tent of Joseph, and did not choose the tribe of Ephraim, but chose the tribe of Judah, Mount Zion which He loved."

In Gen 48:17-20 Joseph took his two sons Manasseh and Ephraim to Jacob to give them his last blessing. Jacob put his right hand on Ephraim's head to give him the blessing of the firstborn. When Joseph protested because Manasseh was the older, Jacob said Ephraim would be the greater.

Num 13:8 Joshua means savior and is the same name in Hebrew as Jesus is in Greek. He was successor to Moses and was from the tribe of Ephraim. He and Caleb brought a good report when they came back from spying out the land, they were the only men that were numbered (over the age of 20 when they left Egypt) that were allowed to go into the land.

Why God would change His plan we can't be sure but in a litany of the shortcomings of the people of Israel in Ps 78, there was a reference to Ephraim.

Ps 78:9 "The children of Ephraim, being armed and carrying bows, turned back in the day of battle." In Judges 1:29 Ephraim did not drive out the Canaanites but lived among them. In Jer 31:18 Ephraim bemoans the chastising of the Lord and in verse 20 the Lord says He will have mercy.

But, forgiveness does not necessarily bring back a missed opportunity.

Day 22 Gen 43-44; Mark 15-16; Ps 106-110; Pr 22

Ps 22:9 "He who has a generous eye will be blessed, for he gives of his bread to the Poor."

Is 55:2 "Why do you spend money for what is not bread, and your wages for what does not satisfy?"

Tim 6:10 "The love of money is the root of all kinds of evil ... "The priorities we put on money always reveals who we really are, how we use it and how we can help others. Your treasure and your heart can not be separated; Mt 6:21

I Tim 5:8 A man who does not provide for his family is not respected by man or God, but most of us don't have to make choices between starving and helping someone in need. The tithe belongs to the Lord and many churches have a program for benevolence, but we should always be alert for people that the Lord brings to us. So many times the ones who need help most will not talk about their situation, let alone ask for help. Watch and pray.

Day 23 Gen 45-46; Luke 1-2; Ps 111-115; Pr 23

The name Jesus means Savior and so does Joshua in the Hebrew. They both had the task of leading their people out of the wilderness of Sin into a land of promise. As we leave the desert of ignorance and begin to follow, the battles come, but not all at once. We have a time of fighting and then a time of rest. Sometimes we will win a battle and sometimes we lose. We will usually have a pause in fighting while we recommit and gather strength to fight either the same enemy or move on to a new territory.

Hebrews 12:1 "Therefore we also, since we are surrounded by so great a cloud of witnesses, let us lay aside every weight, and the sin which so easily ensnares us, and let us run with endurance the race that is set before us," The sin that is so hard for me to overcome may not even be a temptation for you. There are the easy battles and then there those that come back to haunt us over and over. Until the day of our death, we must push on and be vigilant because the old weakness will come around again.

The Essential Word ▮▮▮ 21

Day 24 Gen 47-48; Luke 3-4; Ps 116-120; Pr 24

As Jacob prophesies over his sons, Reuben the firstborn should have received the double portion (birthright and blessing; Esau sold his birthright for a pot of stew and Jacob stole the blessing by trickery) but because Reuben had sexual relations with one of his father's wives, Jacob gave it to Joseph by dividing Ephraim from Manasseh as two separate tribes and separate territories.

I Chronicles 5:1-2 "Now the sons of Reuben the firstborn of Israel---he was indeed the firstborn, but because he defiled his father's bed, his birthright was given to the sons of Joseph, the son of Israel, so that the genealogy is not listed according to the birthright; yet Judah prevailed over his brothers, and from him came a ruler, although the birthright was Joseph's---"

Leah who was so unappreciated in life was honored in death, being buried with Abraham and Sarah, Isaac and Rebekah. His beloved Rachel died in childbirth (Benjamin) and was buried by the way as they traveled to Ephrath. Jacob lived seventeen years after being reunited with Joseph. He was embalmed in Egypt and taken back to be buried with Leah in the cave that had been bought by Abraham.

Day 25 Gen 49-50; Luke 5-6; Ps 121-125; Pr 25

Pr 25:21-22 "If your enemy is hungry, give him bread to eat; and if he is thirsty, give him drink; for so you will heap coals of fire on his head, and the Lord will reward you."

This is the act of the high priest for their atonement.

Num 16:46 "And Moses said to Aaron, 'Take a censer, and put fire in it from off the altar, and lay incense on it, and carry it quickly to the congregation, and make atonement for them, for there is wrath gone out from the Lord;" Rev 8:3-4 incense comes to God with the prayer of the saints.

I Peter 2:9 "But you are a chosen generation, a royal priesthood, a holy nation, His own special people, that you may proclaim the praises of Him who called you out of darkness into His marvelous light."

The high priest (Lev 16:12) stands between the sinner and the judgment of God.

II Cor 5:18 "Now all things are of God, who has reconciled us to Himself through Jesus Christ, and has given us the ministry of reconciliation,"

Day 26 Ex 1-2; Luke 7-8; Ps 126-130; Pr 26

The new king in Egypt had not known Joseph and became afraid of the Israelites because they had become so many. His plan to stop the population growth didn't work to his advantage. The small minds of despots seem to come to similar conclusions like Herod when he killed all the boy babies under two years old. Despots see people as chaff, to be blown away if inconvenient.

God urged Jochebed to put Moses into a crocodile infested river and because she obeyed, he was saved.

When Moses grew up he fled Egypt in fear of being punished for killing an Egyptian. This is a pattern that never gets old. God puts us in a bad situation to draw us into His plan for us. The worst that ever happened to you will very likely be the best thing that ever happened to you because it changed the course of your life. We are always doing the right thing to trust Him with the outcome. (So it took forty years for Moses, we need to be patient).

Jeremiah 29:11 "For I know the thoughts and plans that I have for you, says the Lord, thoughts and plans for welfare and peace, and not for evil, to give you hope in your final outcome." (Amplified Bible)

Day 27 Ex 3-4; Luke 9-10; Ps 131-135; Pr 27

God knows our capabilities better than we do because He gave them to us. We see our flaws and insecurities and He sees our hesitation as lack of trust. All the great heroes of the Bible were just men of "like passions" Acts 14:15.

James 5:17 "Elijah was a human being with a nature such as we have---with feelings, affections and constitution as we ourselves; and he prayed earnestly for it not to rain, and no rain fell on the earth for three years and six months." (I Kings 17:1)

The Lord said to Moses, "Go," and Moses answered with a list of his inadequacies. But God had to show him the way and overcome all Moses' objections.

I Cor 1:27 "But God has chosen the foolish things of the world to put to shame the wise and God has chosen the weak things of the world to put to shame the things which are mighty."

Are you ready to follow God's plan for you without hesitation and excuses?

Rev 7:17 Will you have tears wiped from your eyes when He shows how far you've missed His perfect plan for you? We all fall short but that doesn't mean we shouldn't try.

Day 28 Ex 5-6; Luke 11-12; Ps 136-140; Pr 28

Luke 11:9 Be persistent, do not quit asking until God answers your prayer. When He urges you to pray for someone you know it is His will to move in that time and place. He has made us partners in His plan to save and heal and move the immovable. We want our life to be easier, a better job, more money, lay back and relax. We live in a material society that gets excited about new cars, trips, clothing, and jewelry.

God calls that vanity, empty, false, lying and idolatry. That is not His idea of a better life for us. He wants us to feel the grief and pain of those around us. Pray with intelligence, and with the help of the Holy Spirit. Pray and keep on praying until you get a release, we are fighting Satan and his demons for a soul. We can't just throw a few words into the air and go do something else. Your mother did not stop her travail in labor until your birth was completed. We belong to Him, our time is borrowed from Him.

There is an excellent book; "Praying Effectively for the Lost" that is available at www.pelministries.org

Day 29 Ex 7-8; Luke 13-14; Ps 141-145; Pr 29

Mt 5:45 "He…sends rain on the just and the unjust"…

The plagues were sent on Egypt and everyone in the land suffered. Sometimes God protects people or places for His own reasons. He was ready to show Pharaoh that He could bring disaster on Egypt and protect Israel.

Ex 8:23 "I will make a difference between My people and your people. Tomorrow this sign shall be."

The plagues were; 1. Water changed to blood. 2. Frogs, 3. Lice. The rest of the plagues were on only the Egyptians. 4. Swarms of flies, 5. Livestock dying, 6. Boils, 7. Hail mingled with fire, 8. Locusts, 9. Sun was darkened, 10. Death of the first born.

Ex 9:20-21 Only those Egyptians who believed the words of Moses and brought their servants and livestock inside were safe from the hail.

The people of Egypt had many gods, Ra the sun god, the Nile River, the Pharaoh and his royal linage, and many more. God brought judgment on their idols and showed Himself higher and more powerful than all their gods.

Day 30 Ex 9-10; Luke 15-16; Ps 146-150; Pr 30

Zech 1:3 & 16… "Thus says the Lord of hosts; 'Return to Me … and I will return to you." "I am returning to Jerusalem with mercy."

Zech 3:1-4 "Then he showed me Joshua the high priest standing before the Angel of the Lord, and Satan standing at his right hand to oppose him. And the Lord said to Satan, "The Lord rebuke you Satan! The Lord who has chosen Jerusalem rebuke you! Is this not a brand plucked from the fire?" Now Joshua was clothed with filthy garments, and was standing before the Angel. Then He answered and spoke to those who stood before Him, saying, "Take away the filthy garments from him." And to him He said, "See I have removed your iniquity from you, and I will clothe you with rich robes."

Luke 15:12-22 There is a son who does not like the restraints on his fun and decides to go out and have a good time with his share of the inheritance; though not rightfully his until his father is deceased. He takes his share, one third because the older son gets a double portion; Deut 21:15-17. When he comes to the point of repentance, he turns toward home again and his father is watching and waiting for him.

He is received with joy and celebration.

Our Father is always ready to receive us when we return to Him and give us more blessing than we deserve.

Day 31 Ex 11-12; Luke 17-18; Ps 1-5; Pr 31

Pr 31:10 A virtuous woman knows her purpose in the Kingdom of God, her worth is more than any earthly treasure.

She seeks out wool and flax, wool represents good works, and flax (or linen) represents purity through grace.

The Essential Word ▬ 27

Rev 19:7-8 "Let us be glad and rejoice and give Him glory, for the marriage of the Lamb has come, and his wife has made herself ready. And to her it was granted to be arrayed in fine linen, clean and bright, for the fine linen is the righteous acts of the saints."

We are not saved by works; works are the outcome of a right relationship with God. (James 2:17-18)

Her lamp does not go out by night. (Pr 31:18) Whatever dark trials come into her life she is constant in the Holy Spirit for His Spirit overcomes the dark. She does not fear for her family, they are doubly clothed in scarlet (Pr 31:21). Scarlet represents the blood of Jesus, and we clothe our family with teaching (with word and example), and travailing prayer in the Spirit.

(Special thanks to my dear friend Peggy who studied Pr 31 with me, although this is very condensed.)

Day 32 Ex 13-14; Luke 19-20; Ps 6-10; Pr 1

Moses didn't lead the people into the land of the Philistines for four reasons.

1. Abraham had made a covenant with the Philistines, Gen 21:32.
2. The Philistines were not named as their enemy in Gen 15:19-21.
3. The Israelites were not prepared to go into battle, Ex 13:17.
4. The Lord was not finished humbling Egypt.

Ex14:4 Moses led the people to circle around to make it look as if they were trapped and lead Pharaoh to follow and be destroyed. The water of the Red Sea stood up like a wall on both sides of the dry ground. Pharaoh and his army were so arrogant that they went into this obviously miraculous ground. Arrogance blinds people to the good qualities of others; your intelligence, your compassion, your motives are judged with suspicion. The arrogant will think you would react the same way they would if put in the same situation. Arrogance brings division and takes away peace in your relationships.

Day 33 Ex 15-16; Luke 21-22; Ps 11-15; Pr 2

Sometimes we are attacked because we have sinned and give an opening to the devil; and sometimes to be tried and tested. Peter and Paul were great men of God but it did not protect them from all attack.

Luke 22:31 Satan asked for permission to sift Simon Peter like wheat is sifted, separating the grain from the impurities. Satan does not want our sins to go away, he wants to use them to defeat us and beat us down. We like our impurities, if we didn't they would be gone quickly. The Lord wants to separate us too, but He will not rip our sins away, we have to work out our salvation with soul-searching and gritty determination. Philippians 2:12-13

II Cor 12:7 Paul was given a thorn in the flesh to keep him humble.

Eph 4:27 "Leave no (such) room or foothold for the devil---give no opportunity to him." (Amplified)

II Sam 24:13-14 When David sinned by numbering the people of Israel, God gave him a choice of three judgments, David could have seven years of famine in the land, three months being pursued by his enemies or three days of plague. David chose to fall into the hand of God rather than the hand of man, depending on the mercy of the Lord. When David sinned his people were punished.

Pr 14:34 "Righteousness exalteth a nation; but sin is a reproach to any people.' (KJV)

Day 34 Ex 17-18; Luke 23-24; Ps 16-20; Pr 3

Ex 18:19 Jethro, Moses' father-in-law saw Moses judging the people and saw the burden was too heavy for one man. And the people had to wait a long time for their judgments. Jethro advised Moses to teach the Law to the people so they would know what was expected of them. Then lesser judges were put in charge of small groups. Only greater matters were brought to Moses.

Ex 18:21 "moreover you shall select from all the people able men, such as fear God, men of truth, hating covetousness; and place such over them to be rulers of thousands, rulers of hundreds, rulers of fifties, and rulers of tens." If they didn't get justice they could appeal to the next higher court, maybe as high as Moses. The Law was about reparations and restoring stolen property if possible or something of equal value. Injuries were an eye for an eye, a tooth for a tooth and a life for a life.

Jesus established a different standard.

Mt 5:38-46 Don't resist, if you are slapped turn the other cheek, if someone wants to take away your tunic give them your cloak also! Love is the Law, love your enemies. We were enemies to God before forgiveness changed us. It doesn't mean someone stealing your property is right, but if they ask, our reaction is different from the world.

Day 35 Ex 19-20; John 1-2; Ps 21-25; Pr 4

Malachi 4:5 "Behold, I will send you Elijah the prophet before the coming of the great and dreadful day of the Lord." Israel was promised that Elijah would come before Messiah and the time was right.

Dan 9:25 "Know therefore and understand, that from the going forth of the command to restore and build Jerusalem until Messiah the Prince, there shall be seven weeks and sixty-two weeks;"

Scholars believe a week represents 7 years.

John 1:21-22 People ask John the Baptist if he is Elijah or the Prophet, and he said that he was not.

Why did John deny being the messenger?

Mt 16:17 The truth was to be revealed by the Spirit.

Luke 10:21-22 "In that hour Jesus rejoiced in the Spirit and said, "I thank You, Father, Lord of heaven and earth, that you have hidden these things from the wise and prudent and revealed them to babes. Even so, Father; for so it seemed good in Your sight. All things have been delivered to Me by My Father, and no one knows who the Son is except the Father, and who the Father is except the Son, and the one to whom the Son wills to reveal Him"

Jesus could not reveal Himself as the Christ to everyone because His purpose in coming was to be rejected and die for our sins. He revealed the truth to the few that were chosen to be the seed of the new kingdom.

Day 36 Ex 21-22; John 3-4; Ps 26-30; Pr 5

John 3: 26 John's followers came to him to report that Jesus was baptizing, and people were flocking to Him. They were concerned that Jesus was taking John's ministry away from him.

John 3:29-30 "He who has the bride is the bridegroom; but the friend of the bridegroom, who stands and hears him rejoices greatly because of the bridegroom's voice. Therefore this joy of mine is fulfilled. He must increase, but I must decrease."

John was not concerned that his time in the lime-light was over, his purpose had been completed. In the church one ministry is not more important than another, it is just different.

When building a house, what if the foundation crew didn't want to do work that would be hidden from sight and insisted on working on the roof? Prayer is invisible to the world, but is the foundation for any relevant ministry. After sowing seed the field still looks empty, but new life is on the way.

John 4:36 "And he who reaps receives wages, and gathers fruit for eternal life, that both he who sows and he who reaps may rejoice together."

Day 37 Ex 23-24; John 5-6; Ps 31-35; Pr 6

Pr 6:32 "Whoever commits adultery with a woman lacks understanding; he who does so destroys his own soul." From the beginning God created man and woman to be one flesh as an example of all believers being 'one spirit' clinging to Jesus as our husband. One flesh was not to be separated. Adultery tears apart the marriage relationship, they are no longer one. Some marriages are renewed because the offender repents and the offended one makes a decision to renew the covenant, it is a new marriage because the old marriage was destroyed and no longer exists. Anyone who chooses to remain with an adulterous mate in hope they will repent eventually will suffer much, but that may happen.

Jer3:8-10 & 12 "Then I saw that for all the causes for which backsliding Israel had committed adultery, I had put her away and given her a certificate of divorce; yet her treacherous sister Judah did not fear, but went and played the harlot also. Go and proclaim these words toward the north, and say: Return, backsliding Israel, says the Lord; I will not cause My anger to fall on you. For I am merciful, says the Lord; I will not remain angry forever."

Day 38 Ex 25-26; John 7-8; Ps 36-40; Pr 7

Ps 37:35 "I have seen the wicked in great power, and spreading himself like a native green tree."

Simple minded people admire and even envy the rich and powerful but we must pity them.

Their success may look good but it is temporary.

The Essential Word 33

Mark 10:25 Jesus commented on the difficulty for a rich man to be saved, not impossible but very difficult. Pray for their salvation. We serve the Lord by giving praise and worship to Him and serving others. It is a lot easier to give a few dollars to a person in need than to spend as much time as it takes to pray the arrogant into the kingdom of God.

Rev 3:17 "Because you say, 'I am rich, have become wealthy, and have need of nothing'---and do not know that you are wretched, miserable, poor, blind, and naked----"

II Cor 4:3-4 "But even if our gospel is veiled, it is veiled to those who are perishing, whose minds the god of this age has blinded who do not believe, …"

Eph 2:1 Prayer is the only way to bring them to the light, birthing their spirit, so they are no longer dead but alive.

Day 39 Ex 27-28; John 9-10; Ps 41-45; Pr 8

Pr 8:13 "The fear of the Lord is to hate evil; pride and arrogancy, and the evil way, and the froward mouth, do I hate." (KJV)

Heb 12:28-29 "Therefore since we are receiving a kingdom which cannot be shaken, let us have grace by which we may serve God acceptably with reverence and godly fear. For our God is a consuming fire." We are told to love God and trust Him, but we should also fear Him, don't think we can take Him for granted. Like an earthly husband, He expects to be in our thoughts and plans every day, not just Sunday. Give us this day, Jesus, He is our daily Bread.

Ps 34:1 & 7 "I will bless the Lord at all times; His praise shall continually be in my mouth. The Angel of the Lord encamps around those who fear Him--- who revere and worship Him with awe; and each of them He delivers." (Amplified Bible)

Job 28:28 "And unto man he said, Behold, the fear of the Lord, that is wisdom; and to depart from evil is understanding." (KJV)

Day 40 Ex 29-30; John 11-12; Ps 46-50; Pr 9

Ex 30:20 "When they go into the tabernacle of meeting, or when they come near the altar to minister, to burn an offering made by fire to the Lord, they shall wash with water, lest they die."

When Pilate saw the Jews were determined to kill Jesus he, "took water and washed his hands before the multitude, saying, 'I am innocent of the blood of this person." See Ps 26:6

I Cor 6:9-11 "Do you not know that the unrighteous will not inherit the kingdom of God? Do not be deceived. Neither fornicators, nor idolaters, nor adulterers, nor homosexuals, nor sodomites, nor thieves, nor covetous, nor drunkards, nor revilers, nor extortioners will inherit the kingdom of God. And such were some of you. But you were washed, but you were sanctified, but you were justified in the name of the Lord Jesus and by the Spirit of our God."

The Essential Word

Day 41 Ex 31-32; John 13-14; Ps 51-55; Pr 10

Ex 31:2-3 "See I have called by name Bezalel the son of Uri, the son of Hur, of the tribe of Judah. And I have filled him with the Spirit of God in wisdom, in understanding, in knowledge, and in all manner of workmanship,"

He has given us everything we need to complete the work He has assigned to us. Everyone has a ministry that has been made for them.

II Chr 32:7 "Be strong and courageous; do not be afraid nor dismayed …."

II Tim 1:12 …"for I know whom I have believed and am persuaded that He is able to keep what I have committed to Him until that Day."

Isaiah 43:1-2 …"Fear not, for I have redeemed you; I have called you by your name; you are Mine. When you pass through the waters, I will be with you; and through the rivers, they shall not overflow you. When you walk through the fire, you shall not be burned, nor the flame scorch you."

Do not fear man, he can only destroy your flesh, fear God and serve Him with joy.

Day 42 Ex 33-34; John 15-16; Ps 56-60; Pr 11

Ex 34:12-14 "Take heed to yourself, lest you make a covenant with the inhabitants of the land where you are going, lest it be a snare in your midst. But you shall destroy their altars, break their sacred pillars, and cut down their wooden images (for you shall worship no other god, for the Lord whose name is Jealous, is a jealous God)." The inhabitants were to be totally removed from the Land, their places of idol worship destroyed.

God knew that the pull of the sin nature would draw Israel into idolatry, if these places were left. Strong demons were worshiped in the groves. There were both male and female prostitutes, often very young placed there for the perverted pleasure of "worshipers." Asherah was a fertility goddess considered to be the wife of Baal.

Molech and Chemosh were represented with ugly statues with a place for fire, built for the sacrifice of babies and small children. Satan so hates innocence that he often urges his followers to torture or kill infants and children.

Day 43 Ex 35-36; John 17-18; Ps 61-65; Pr 12

Everyone who was willing brought the materials for the tabernacle and had to be restrained from bringing more because Bezalel and Aholiab told Moses they had more than enough to finish the work. God's presence was with them in a cloud by day and a pillar of fire by night and yet how easy was it to take Him for granted.

Unity of purpose is the difference between success and failure.

Gen 11:6 "Indeed the people are one, and they have one language, and this is what they begin to do; now nothing that they propose to do will be withheld from them."

I Cor 1:10 "Now I plead with you, brethren, by the name of our Lord Jesus Christ, that you all speak the same thing, and that there be no divisions among you, but that you be perfectly joined together in the same mind and in the same judgment."

Jn 17:22 "And the glory which You gave Me I have given them, that they may be one just as We are one."

Day 44 Ex 37-38; John 19-20; Ps 66-70; Pr 13

John 20:21-23 "So Jesus said to them again, Peace to you! (Just) as the Father has sent Me forth so I am sending you and having said this, He breathed on (them) and said to them, Receive (admit) the Holy Spirit! [Now having received the Holy Spirit and being led and directed by Him] if you forgive the sins of any one they are forgiven; if you retain the sins of any one, they are retained." (Amplified Bible)

If we don't forgive that person who hurts us, they are not forgiven!

Mark 9:42 "And whoever causes one of (these believers) these little ones who acknowledge and cleave to Me to stumble and sin, it would be better --- more profitable and wholesome --- for him if a (huge) millstone were hung about his neck, and he were thrown into the sea." (Amplified)

We have forgiveness from God and with it comes heavy responsibility. When we are offended and carry that offence and revisit it and talk about it, even in our own thoughts, we are sinning. Jesus came to reconcile sinners to Himself and we need to take very seriously binding the cords of judgment on anyone just because we got our feelings hurt.

Eph 4:26...do not let the sun go down on your wrath.

II Cor 5:10 "For we must all appear before the judgment seat of Christ, that each one may receive the things done in the body, according to what he has done, whether good or bad."

I Cor 3:15 "If anyone's work is burned, he will suffer loss; but he himself will be saved, yet so as through fire."

Although I can't send one to Hell by unforgiveness, that one who made me stumble and I will both be accountable at the judgment seat of Christ.

Day 45 Ex 39-40; John 21-Acts 1; Ps 71-75; Pr 14

Ex 40 Moses set up the tabernacle. He had no help because the priests were not yet anointed for the service. The cross is in the layout of the tabernacle. Moses had seen the pattern in Heaven and he understood the ultimate sacrifice which would be revealed in shadow throughout his lifetime.

After the tabernacle was finished Moses brought Aaron and his sons to be prepared for service. They came by way of the altar of sacrifice; their sin had to be covered by blood. They were washed; clean from sin and anointed; with oil representing the baptism of the Holy Spirit. Then they were ready to serve as priests, to stand between God's judgment and the Israelites.

Heb 9:22 "And according to the law almost all things are purified with blood, and without shedding of blood there is no remission."

Day 46 Lev 1-2; Acts 2-3; Ps 76-80; Pr 15

You will bring a sacrifice without blemish from your flock, it must be something of value to you. Not a diseased or crippled animal that probably was going to die anyway.

Lev 1:2-4 "Then he shall put his hand on the head of the burnt offering and it will be accepted on his behalf to make atonement for him."

I Peter 1:18-20 "knowing that you were not redeemed with corruptible things, like silver or gold, from your aimless conduct received by tradition from your fathers, but with the precious blood of Christ, as of a lamb without blemish and without spot. He indeed was foreordained before the foundation of the world, but was manifest in these last times for you."

Jesus was the perfect lamb that was bound to earth, not by the power of man or nature, but by the will of God.

Day 47 Lev 3-4; Acts 4-5; Ps 81-85; Pr 16

Peter and John spoke boldly to the High priest and would not go quietly into obscurity. Their message was too important.

Acts 4:29 "Now, Lord, look on their threats, and grant to Your servants that with all boldness they may speak Your word" And the building was shaken and they were filled with the Holy Spirit and with boldness and they were one heart and soul. Then they had the power of unity to turn their world upside down. Gen 11: God spoke on the power of unity (Day 6) for good or evil.

Ananias and his wife Sapphira wanted to pretend they were unified with the church. When they sold property they were free to keep all the money, give all the money, or give a portion. They wanted the church to think highly of them and lied to Peter. Pretended unity does not make strength. The American Church is powerless because we have not faced persecution. We think we are persecuted if people don't agree with us. When we face death for our faith then we will learn how strong or weak we are. When we face death for our faith we will learn who the true believers are. Persecution is not enjoyable but it makes giants of ordinary men, women and even children.

Mark 4:16-17 "These likewise are the ones sown on stony ground who, when they hear the word, immediately receive it with gladness; and they have no root in themselves, and so endure only for a time. Afterward when tribulation or persecution arises for the word's sake, immediately they stumble." Persecution will change you; you will be stronger or give up.

Day 48 Lev 5-6; Acts 6-7; Ps 86-90; Pr 17

Acts 6:1 Even in the congregation of the early church there arose a complaint. The Hebrew speaking widows were getting food but the Hellenists; Greek speaking widows; were not. The leaders needed to give their time to prayer and to the ministry of the word. So, as with Moses the leaders had to be relieved of the everyday tasks. Men were chosen to do the work and the church grew.

Stephen was chosen for what some would think is a menial, low class job, but he accepted because he was thankful to be used by the Lord. His spirit was not envious and he did great wonders and miracles. Men tried to argue with him as he preached but they couldn't win any argument against him. I can imagine them nodding their heads as he talks about their history but then he rebuked them for idolatry. As Stephen was dying he asked for forgiveness for his killers, repeating the words of Jesus.

Day 49 Lev 7-8; Acts 8-9; Ps 91-95; Pr 18

The message of the church was spread by persecution. Rome allowed conquered people to keep their religion. As long as tribute was taken back to Rome the people could worship any gods they preferred, this kept the peoples from revolt as the Empire grew. The Pharisees had lost the power they had over the civil government, (they could request but not demand), but still had a lot of power over the realm of worship. They had respect from the people and were supported from the offerings brought to the Temple.

Christians were a threat because they did not need to bring offerings to the Temple since Jesus was the final sacrifice. As Christians tried to escape imprisonment and beatings, God's purpose was fulfilled. Everywhere the Church went, the Good News was spread. Persecution will separate the true believers from those who cannot stand in times of trouble.

After Simon (the sorcerer) believed and was baptized, he revealed that his heart was not right when he wanted to pay for the gift of the Holy Spirit. The church was kept pure through the revelation of the Holy Spirit.

When Constantine declared the Roman Empire Christian about 325 AD, he brought the church under the influence of the Roman government which stopped the apostolic fervor.

Day 50 Lev 9-10; Acts 10-11; Ps 96-100; Pr 19

Lev 10:1-2 Nadab and Abihu died quickly for not following the pattern exactly. Were they trying to please God in their own way? God's pattern was so precise because everything they did had to point to Jesus. Moses saw the pattern in Heaven and the table of showbread went right here and the laver for washing was exactly there.

Nadab and Abihu were killed by fire from the Lord, but they were carried out by their tunics (their clothes were not destroyed). Their cousins were called in to remove the bodies for the priests were not allowed to touch unclean things. Aaron and his remaining sons were told not to mourn by tearing their clothes and uncovering their heads or they would die also.

Num 18:12 "All the best of the oil, all the best of the new wine and the grain, their firstfruits which they offer to the Lord, I have given them to you."

Lev 10:9 God speaks to Aaron, "Do not drink wine or intoxicating drink, you, nor your sons with you, when you go into the tabernacle of meeting, lest you die. It shall be a statute forever throughout your generations, that you may distinguish between holy and unholy," This is the first time God mentions wine in connection with the tabernacle, so it can be inferred that Nadab and Abihu may have been drinking.

Day 51 Lev 11-12; Acts 12-13; Ps 101-105; Pr 20

Acts 12:21-23 Herod came to Caesarea and gave an oration and the people shouted, "The voice of a god and not a man!" An angel struck him and he was eaten by worms and died because he accepted worship that belongs only to God.

I Sam 3:11-14; & 4:18 Eli knew that his sons were doing evil things but did not stop them. And when he heard that the ark was taken and his sons were dead, he fell backwards, broke his neck and died.

I Sam 25:15-18 David being pursued by Saul went to the wilderness of Paran. A wealthy man, Nabal, was shearing sheep. David and his men had helped Nabal's men to protect the sheep. David sent and asked for food for his men and Nabal rudely refused, breaking the custom of hospitality. Nabal's wife Abigail went to David and asked for mercy. When Nabal heard what Abigail had done his heart died within him and he lay as a stone for 10 days and died.

Heb 9:27 "And as it is appointed for men to die once, but after this the judgment,"

There comes a time when you have no more chances to repent.

Day 52 Lev 13-14; Acts 14-15; Ps 106-110; Pr 21

Acts 14:22..."We must through many tribulations enter the kingdom of God."

Paul knew about tribulations.

II Cor 11:24-27 He said, "From the Jews five times I received forty stripes minus one. Three times I was beaten with rods; once I was stoned; three times I was shipwrecked; a night and a day I have been in the deep; in journeys often, in perils of waters, in perils of robbers, in perils of my own countrymen, in perils of the gentiles, in perils in the city, in perils in the wilderness, in perils in the sea, in perils among false brethren; in weariness and toil, in sleeplessness often, in hunger and thirst in fastings often, in cold and nakedness. ..."

Paul joined with the other Pharisees to persecute the young church. When he defected and turned away from what he had formerly believed, their anger burned more strongly against him than all the others.

Day 53 Lev 15-16; Acts 16-17; Ps 111-115; Pr 22

Pr 22:20-21 "Have I not written to you excellent things of counsels and knowledge, that I may make you know the certainty of the words of truth, that you may answer words of truth to those who send to you?"

The Lord has placed us to be His witness to the lost around us, to reflect his light and his glory. Jesus is the light of the world and people we see or meet every day will see Him in our lives. They need His peace and comfort as they live this day and salvation for eternity.

We witness every minute by actions and reactions and I know that words from my mouth have reflected poorly on the Lord. Lord, help us to find the words He wants us to say to draw a friend to understand. Be sensitive to the Holy Spirit and feel his leading. Whether that person needs a word of comfort or a rebuke, He will guide you. But the first thing is to pray for them before a word comes from your mouth.

II Peter 3:15 "But sanctify the Lord God in your hearts, and always be ready to give a defense to everyone who asks you a reason for the hope that is in you, with meekness and fear;"

Day 54 Lev 17-18; Acts 18-19; Ps 116-120; Pr 23

It is better to repent quickly.

Ps 119:67 "Before I was afflicted I went astray, but now I keep Your word."

Judges 6:1 & 4 "Then the children of Israel did evil in the sight of the Lord. So the Lord delivered them into the hand of Midian for seven years. …. The enemy would encamp against them and destroy the produce of the earth as far as Gaza, and leave no sustenance for Israel, neither sheep nor ox nor donkey."

Ps 119:71 "It is good for me that I have been afflicted, that I may learn your statutes.

Jer 26:3 "Perhaps everyone will listen and turn from his evil way, that I may relent concerning the calamity which I purpose to bring on them because of the evil of their doings."

Ps 119:75 "I know, O Lord, that Your judgments are right, and that in faithfulness You have afflicted me."

Jer 3:12 "Return, backsliding Israel,' says the Lord; 'I will not cause My anger to fall on you. For I am merciful, says the Lord; I will not remain angry forever."

God does not do things on a whim. As a shepherd works to keep His sheep from deep water or the cliffs edge, He is always keeping watch over us. He may have to give a sharp whack to keep us from stubbornly going our own way.

Day 55 Lev 19-20; Acts 20-21; Ps 121-125; Pr 24

Our help comes from the Lord. If we obey, we are blessed, but often what seems like a curse is a blessing in disguise.

Ps 121 This chapter is all about being protected and kept safe. He is watching always, He does not take a nap and let us fend for ourselves, but the world is corrupt and evil surrounds us. Our flesh leans toward disobedience at all times and the devil stalks around the earth looking for those he can devour. (I Peter 5:8)

Romans 8:22 "For we know that the whole creation groans and labors with birth pangs together until now." We are in a battlefield and fighting never ceases. We can't afford to be slack about obeying God.

Luke 12:39 "But know this, that if the master of the house had known what hour the thief would come, he would have watched and not allowed his house to be broken into."

The Essential Word   47

Matt 26:41 "Watch and pray, lest you enter into temptation. The spirit indeed is willing, but the flesh is weak."

I Peter 4:18-19 "If the righteous one is scarcely saved, where will the ungodly and the sinner appear?"

Pr 11:31 "Therefore let those who suffer according to the will of God commit their souls to Him in doing good, as to a faithful Creator."

Whatever we face, He can be trusted to bring us through.

Day 56 Lev 21-22; Acts 22-23; Ps 126-130; Pr 25

Acts 23:7-8 Pharisees and Sadducees disagreed about the resurrection. The Sadducees were not believers in anything spiritual, resurrection of the dead, angels or demons, anything in the spirit realm; you have to wonder on what they based their religion. The Sadducees believed in the strict adherence to the Law of Moses; the Pharisees believed in the written law but also in the oral law.

Ex 31:15 "Work shall be done for six days, but the seventh is the Sabbath of rest, holy to the Lord, Whoever does any work on the Sabbath day, he shall surely be put to death."

Acts 1:12, there is a reference to a Sabbath day's journey. This was added to the written Law and became part of the tradition. The guardians of the Law had become Law writers.

Mt 23:4 "For they bind heavy burdens, hard to bear, and lay them on men's shoulders; but they themselves will not move them with one of their fingers."

Day 57 Lev 23-24; Acts 24-25; Ps 131-135; Pr 26

Pr 26:11 "As a dog returns to his own vomit, so a fool repeats his folly."

How many resolutions and decisions and promises have we given to others or to ourselves have we broken? Over and over have I planned to get up early and read my Bible, spend time praying for some ones salvation, eat better, lose weight, the list is endless. The selfishness of our sin nature pulls us so strongly; we seem to be caught in a rip tide with no way out.

Paul understood this very well.

Rom 7:22-23 "For I delight in the Law of God according to the inward man. But I see another law in my members, warring against the law of my mind, and bringing me into captivity to the law of sin which is in my members"

But there is hope.

Ps 119:25 &11 "My soul clings to the dust, revive me according to Your word. Your word I have hidden in my heart, that I might not sin against You."

David was a man who knew his own weakness but trusted God to be his "strength and shield." Ps 28:7 Ps 1:1-2 "Blessed is the man who walks not in the counsel of the ungodly, nor stands in the path of sinners, nor sits in the seat of the scornful; but his delight is in the law of the Lord, and in His law he meditates day and night."

The Word of God is our hope and strength; study and keep your thoughts under control, meditate on His love and goodness day and night.

Day 58 Lev 25-26; Acts 26-27; Ps 136-140; Pr 27

Lev 26 God promises to reward obedience with rain and plentiful crops, peace in the land and victory over their enemies. Sin will be punished by disease, hunger and being defeated by their enemies. If that does not bring them back to the Lord, then it will be 7 times more. If they remain stubborn, then it really gets bad. But the Lord will not forget His covenant and is eager to forgive and restore if they are humbled and accept their guilt.

II Chr 7:13-14 "When I shut up heaven and there is no rain, or command the locusts to devour the land, or send pestilence among My people, if My people who are called by My name will humble themselves, and pray and seek My face, and turn from their wicked ways, then will I hear from heaven, and will forgive their sin and heal their land."

Some might call it Karma; we call it reaping what you have sown.

Hosea 8:7 "They sow the wind, and reap the whirlwind. The stalk has no bud; it shall never produce meal, if it should produce, aliens would swallow it up."

The Lord is just, He does not punish without reason.

Day 59 Lev 27-Num 1; Acts 28-Rom 1; Ps 141-145; Pr 28

Rom 1:18 & 21 "For the wrath of God is revealed from heaven against all ungodliness and unrighteousness of men, who suppress the truth in unrighteousness, because, although they knew God, they did not glorify Him as God, nor were thankful, but became futile in their thoughts, and their foolish hearts were darkened."

Nature abhors a vacuum. When we reject the truth we will believe lies. One of the most important truths is that we need to always be thankful to God for His mercy, because if we do not our minds and hearts are darkened and all kinds of sins arise; envy, bitterness, covetousness, lust. Judah is the same word meaning exuberant praise as the word that is translated thankful in Romans 1:21. Being thankful is not a passive thing. Being thankful is active and aggressive moving us toward being the warriors we are meant to be, tearing down the strongholds of darkness.

Day 60 Num 2-3; Rom 2-3; Ps 146-150; Pr 29

Ps 147:15 "He sends out His command to the earth; His word runs very swiftly."

The Essential Word 51

The purpose of the Law is to reveal to us our own sin nature. When we judge ourselves against the behavior of others we can congratulate ourselves on how good we are.

We think, I do this, but I would never do that. We judge others whose sins are more serious than ours in our own minds. We delude ourselves into thinking our sin is of no significance, God does not grade on the curve.

Romans 12:2 "And do not be conformed to this world, but be transformed by the renewing of your mind, that you may prove what is that good and acceptable and perfect will of God."

The Law also was to keep them healthy and protect Israel against the diseases prevalent in a land filled with perverted worship of idols. This is the reason most of the indigenous tribes had to be destroyed including children, animals and clothing.

Day 61 Num 4-6; Rom 4-5; Ps 1-3; Pr 30

Rom 4:3 "Abraham believed God, and it was accounted to him for righteousness."

Circumcision in the flesh is the outward sign of belonging to God, but the outward sign is not enough. The heart must believe. Abraham was ninety when he was commanded to circumcise all his males, including the four year old Ishmael. How was Abraham saved before Jesus died for our sin?

Rom 1:20 "For since the creation of the world His invisible attributes are clearly seen, being understood by the things that are made, even His eternal power and Godhead, so that they are without excuse,"

Ps 19:1-2 "The heavens declare the glory of God; and the firmament shows His handiwork. Day unto day utters speech, and night unto night reveals knowledge."

Every people and culture have worshiped. From Aztec pyramids and shrines to statues of various idols, there are signs of religious ceremonies. Man is compelled to worship. How do we find the true God?

Rom 2:14-15 "for when Gentiles, who do not have the law, by nature do the things in the law, these, although not having the law, are a law to themselves, who show the work of the law written in their hearts, their conscience also bearing witness, and between themselves their thoughts accusing or else excusing them"

Day 62 Num 7-9; Rom 6-7; Ps 4-6; Pr 31

Num 9:15-16 "Now on the day that the tabernacle was raised up, the cloud covered the tabernacle, the tent of the Testimony; from evening until morning it was above the tabernacle like the appearance of fire. So it was always; the cloud covered it by day, and the appearance of fire by night."

Num 9:22 "Whether it was two days, a month, or a year that the cloud remained above the tabernacle, the children of Israel would remain encamped and not journey; but when it was taken up, they would journey."

The Essential Word ▖▖ 53

What an awesome sight it had to be! There were 603,550 men aged 20 and older that were able for war and only God knows how many old men, women, children and animals, plus the Levites spread out around a tabernacle of worship. They were lined up by families to the east, west, north and south. If you were able to fly over you would see that they were in the shape of the cross facing east.

Day 63 Num 10-12; Rom 8-9; Ps 7-9; Eccl 1

The people were thrilled with manna in the beginning, but just as we take things for granted their gratitude turned to grumbling.

Num 11:5 "We remember the fish which we ate freely in Egypt, the cucumbers, the melons, the leeks, the onions, and garlic; but now our whole being is dried up; there is nothing at all except this manna before our eyes!"

Rom 10:21(Is 65:1) "All day long I have stretched out My hands to a disobedient and contrary people."

Num 11:1 The people had been wandering in the desert for well over two years and were living in the power of the flesh and not in the power of the Holy Spirit. This is not a viable excuse and they were punished, but when I think of how my flesh cries out if I decide to fast for a few days, I have no room for condemning them.

Day 64 Num 13-15; Rom 10-11; Ps 10-12; Eccl 2;

Num 13 Spies were sent into the land. Ten of them brought back a report that discouraged the people. The enemy is too big, too strong; the cities fortified, blah, blah, blah. Of course the enemy was big and strong, what do we need the Lord for if we can handle everything by ourselves? Why have Jesus die if we can be righteous by just trying hard enough? We should be small in our own eyes and trust the Lord to save us.

Caleb and Joshua tried to change their minds but fear had already taken them captive.

Num 14:8-9 "If the Lord delights in us, then He will bring us into this land and give it to us,...Only do not rebel against the Lord, nor fear the people of the land, for they are our bread; their protection has departed from them and the Lord is with us. Do not fear them." When Joshua and Caleb were about to be stoned the glory of the Lord appeared. (Day 8 tells about the enemies in the land, and Hittite means fear, discourage, terrify, etc.)

God was ready for the second time to wipe out the lot of them and make a great nation of Moses, but Moses asked for their lives.

Num 14:17-19 & 37 Because of their bad report the ten spies who brought the bad report, died by the plague, and the men who rebelled were condemned to die in the wilderness, this began the 40 years of wandering.

Day 65 Num 16-18; Rom 12-13; Ps 13-15; Eccl 3

Rom 12:4, 5 & 16 "For as we have many members in one body, but all the members do not have the same function, so we, being many, are one body....... Be of the same mind toward one another. Do not set your mind on high things, but associate with the humble. Do not be wise in your own opinion." Num 16 Some Levites and Reubenites gathered together against Moses and Aaron, asking them, "Why do you exalt yourselves above the assembly of the Lord?" These rebels were punished in a dramatic way and Aaron had to run between the living and the dead to stop the plague that struck, killing 14,700 people.

Num 17:8 The Lord shows that Aaron and his sons were His choice for ministry by making Aaron's rod by the next morning sprout buds, blossoms and ripe almonds.

Num 18:1 "Then the Lord said to Aaron; "You and your sons and your father's house with you shall bear the iniquity related to the sanctuary,..."

Like Jesus, Aaron was to bear the sin for the people.

And, as we are forgiven but keep our sin nature, so were they. If an unclean insect touched them while they slept, they were unclean; they had to be aware that they had to come to be cleansed again and again and again and again.

Day 66 Num 19-21; Rom 14-15; Ps 16-18; Eccl 4

Num 20:17 Moses asks for permission to go through the territory of Edom (Esau), and was denied

Edom said, "you shall not pass through." Edom came out against Israel with many men and since Edom was their brother they turned away and respected his border.

Deut 2:4-5 "...You are about to pass through the territory of your brethren, the descendants of Esau, who live in Seir; and they will be afraid of you. Therefore watch yourselves carefully. Do not meddle with them, for I will not give you any of their land, no, not so much as one footstep, because I have given Mount Seir to Esau as a possession."

God is faithful to His promise.

When Israel came to the land of the Amorites they asked for permission to go through, promising to not eat from their fields or drink from their wells. The king came against them and Israel defeated them and lived in their cities.

Day 67 Num 22-24; Rom 16-I Cor 1; Ps 19-21; Eccl 5

I Cor 1:10 "Now I plead with you, brethren, by the name of our Lord Jesus Christ, that you all speak the same thing, and that there be no divisions among you, but that you be perfectly joined together in the same mind and in the same judgment."

Paul was concerned by the divisions in the Church (Rom 16:17 he warns against those who cause them). The devil will lead off the narrow way with deception. He spoke true words to Eve when he said; Gen 3:5 "For God knows that in the day you eat of it your eyes will be opened, and you will be like God, knowing good from evil." With a twist he told the truth and a lie at the same time. He even quoted God's Word when he tempted Jesus, Mt 4:6. Divisions in the Church have caused us to

The Essential Word ▌▌▌ 57

have less power to change the world. The world sees a splintered group, who often are more concerned with their doctrines and teachings being right than with saving lost souls.

Day 68 Num 25-27; I Cor 2-3; Ps 22-24; Eccl 6

Ps 23 …"for You are with me; Your rod and Your staff, they comfort me."

The rod and staff are for correction and guidance (driving and leading.) Both tools are from love.

The definitions of these words from Strong's concordance are:

Rod: from 7626: to branch off; a scion; --a stick (for punishing, writing, fighting, ruling, walking, rod, sceptre.)

Staff: from 4938: support, protect, sustenance, stay. From 8172: lean, lie, rely, rest, stay.

Ps 31:3 He is my Rock (to cling to) and my fortress; (to surround and protect) He leads me and guides me for His names sake.

Pr 13:24 "He who spares his rod hates his son, but he who loves him disciplines him promptly."

(Also read, Pr 22:15; 23:13-14; 29:15)

Day 69 Num 28-30; I Cor 4-5; Ps 25-27; Eccl 7

I Cor 10:1-4 "Moreover, brethren, I do not want you to be unaware that all our fathers were under the cloud, all passed through the sea, all were baptized into Moses in the cloud and in the sea, all ate the same spiritual food, and all drank the same spiritual drink. For they drank of that spiritual Rock that followed them, and that Rock was Christ."

Moses and David, both knew there would be a future resurrection.

Ps 81:10 David sang to the Lord. Under the inspiration of the Holy Spirit he let the Lord fill his mouth with praise and he understood the plan of salvation.

Ps 27:1 "The Lord is my light and my salvation; whom shall I fear? The Lord is the strength of my life; of whom shall I be afraid?"

II Sam 12: 22-23 "And he said, 'While the child was still alive, I fasted and wept;' for I said, 'Who knows, the Lord may be gracious to me, that the child may live.' "But now he is dead; why should I fast? Can I bring him back again? I shall go to him, but he shall not return to me."

He knew there was a resurrection for him and the first child of Bathsheba.

Day 70 Num 31-33; I Cor 6-7; Ps 28-30; Eccl 8

Num 25:1-3 Baal was a demon that was worshiped by acts of prostitution. Israel committed harlotry and bowed down to Baal and worshiped him, (joined to Baal as in marriage). The guilty were killed, but then a man took a Midianite woman into his tent and a priest took a javelin and thrust it through them. The plague that had killed 24,000 was stopped.

Num 31 Israel is told to take vengeance for the Lord and kill every Midianite. They killed all the males. But they kept the women and children. Moses was angry with them; v 16: "Look, these women caused the children of Israel through the council of Balaam, to trespass against the Lord in the incident of Peor…" (Num 23:28)

Demons have strong power to draw men through the lust of the eyes. This is the reason Jesus said:

Mt 5:28-29 "But I say to you that whoever looks at a woman to lust for her has already committed adultery with her in his heart. If your right eye causes you to sin pluck it out and cast it from you for it is more profitable for you that one of your members perish, than for your whole body to be cast into hell."

First the men of Israel were punished, then later Midian.

Day 71 Num 34-36; I Cor 8-9; Ps 31-33; Eccl 9

Num 34 The boundaries laid out by God were enormous compared to the small country that is Israel today, in 2014.

Joshua 1:3-4 "Every place that the sole of your foot will tread upon I have given you, as I said to Moses. From the wilderness and this Lebanon as far as the great river, the River Euphrates, all the land of the Hittites, and to the Great Sea toward the going down of the sun, shall be your territory."

Num 35:6 & 15 & 33 "Now among the cities which you will give to the Levites you shall appoint six cities of refuge, to which a manslayer may flee." "These six cities shall be for refuge for the children of Israel, for the stranger, and for the sojourner among them, that anyone who kills a person accidentally may flee there." If a man strikes someone with a tool of iron or a stone, or in anger he is a murderer and shall be put to death. "So you shall not pollute the land where you are for blood defiles the land, and no atonement can be made for the land, for the blood that is shed on it, except by the blood of him who shed it."

The avenger of the blood is the nearest kinsman and it is his duty to put that man to death. If the death was accidental the slayer may stay in that city until the death of the high priest. Avenger or revenger; is the same word meaning: brother redeemer, which is what Jesus is for us. He drives us to the refuge of the Father.

Day 72 De 1-3; I Cor 10-11; Ps 34-36; Eccl 10

Esau was a robust man, living his life as a hunter going boldly out to bring home game. Favorite of his father and not thinking about his future, he lived for the gratification of the moment. He came home, (after I assume an unsuccessful hunt) tired and very hungry. He was not going to have the meat that he and his father loved. There was Jacob cooking a thick savory soup, the aroma must have been very enticing. Esau was into instant gratification and the birthright was way out there in time. Hunger was now. He regretted later the loss of his birthright, later when his stomach was full. When Jacob stole his blessing, murderous rage filled his heart.

Jacob ran away to the homeland of his mother and was there 21 years. When Jacob came near his homeland again he trembled at the thought

The Essential Word ▏▎ 61

of the anger and threats of Esau. But, Esau ran to meet him fell on his neck weeping and kissing Jacob. Twenty-one years had changed Esau and he welcomed his brother joyfully. When he saw the land was too small for all their people and livestock, Esau moved away to Mt Seir. Gen 36:6-8

De 2:4-6 Moses is instructed to be careful to not provoke the sons of Esau. They were to pay for any food and water they used, because all the land of Mt Seir belonged to their kinsmen.

Day 73 De 4-6; I Cor 12-13; Ps 37-39; Eccl 11

We are all here for a short time.

Ps 37:14 & 35 "The wicked have drawn the sword and have bent their bow, to cast down the poor and needy,... I have seen the wicked in great power, and spreading himself like a native green tree. Yet he passed away, and behold, he was no more;"

Ps 39: 6 "Surely every man walks about like a shadow; surely they busy themselves in vain; he heaps up riches, and does not know who will gather them,"

The wicked lust for power and money; money gives them power and power gives them more money. And what is their end? They die and leave it all behind.

Mt 6:20 "but lay up for yourselves treasures in heaven, where neither moth nor rust destroys and where thieves do not break in and steal,"

The believer in Jesus has riches that he takes with him, and yet leaves behind an inheritance that is shared by many.

Day 74 De 7-9; I Cor 14-15; Ps 40-42; Eccl 12

De 7:1-2 "When the Lord your God brings you into the land which you go to possess, and has cast out many nations before you, the Hittites and the Girgashites and the Amorites and the Canaanites and the Perizzites and the Hivites and the Jebusites, seven nations greater and mightier than you, and when the Lord your God delivers them over to you, you shall conquer them and utterly destroy them. You shall make no covenant with them nor show mercy to them."

On Day 8, I showed the meaning of these names. These enemies can be defeated and we must fight to free others from their power also. Don't give them a back room in your house, destroy them altogether. The Hittite is fear and a giant. We are so prone to give in to Fear, he is strong and more powerful than we are, but Jesus is more powerful than he, and He is on our side.

Day 75 De 10-12 I Cor 16-II Cor 1; Ps 43-45; Song of Solomon 1

The purpose of obedience is to give us strength. Obedience joins us to the power of God, disobedience separates us from God and we have to depend on our own puny strength.

Ps 44: 1-3 & 8 "... O God, our fathers have told us, the deeds You did in their days, in days of old: You drove out the nations with Your hand,.... For they did not gain possession of the land by their own sword, nor did their arm save them; but it was Your right hand, Your arm, and the light of Your countenance, because You favored them.... In God we boast all day long, and praise Your name forever."

I Ps 44:5-6 "Through Thee we will push down our enemies: through Thy name will we tread them under that rise up against us. For I will not trust in my bow, neither shall my sword save me." (KJV)

Day 76 De 13-15; II Cor 2-3; Ps 46-48; Song 2

De 13:6 & 9 If anyone tried to lead you to worship other gods, they must be put death; even your son, your wife, or friend, to remove sin from the camp. This sounds harsh, but before they died they had time to repent. If they don't repent when they know they are about to die, they are very stubborn indeed. You, the person they tried to trap, are to cast the first stone.

In John 8:7 Jesus said, "He who is without sin among you, let him throw a stone at her first." They told Jesus that the woman was caught in the act of adultery and was condemned under the law. Jesus was the only man there who was without sin, but He had a different mission.

John 3:17 "For God did not send His Son into the world to condemn the world, but that the world through Him might be saved."

II Cor 3:5-6 "Not that we are sufficient of ourselves to think of anything as being from ourselves, but our sufficiency is from God, who also made us sufficient as ministers of the new covenant, not of the letter but of the Spirit for the letter kills, but the Spirit gives life."

Day 77 De 16-18; II Cor 4-5; Ps 49-51; Song 3

De 17:6 "Whoever is deserving of death shall be put to death on the testimony of two or three witnesses; he shall not be put to death on the testimony of one witness."

II Cor 13:1 "This will be the third time I am coming to you. 'By the mouth of two or three witnesses every word shall be established.'"

Rev 22:17 "And the Spirit and the bride say, 'Come!' And let him who hears say, 'Come!' And let him who thirsts come. Whoever desires, let him take the water of life freely."

The sinner is drawn to God by the Spirit and the witness of the Church. The witness of the Church is service through love. A judgmental attitude even when it is unspoken is clear. If you can't love them in the flesh, love them in the Spirit. We don't love them because they deserve it; we love them because God loves them.

Day 78 De 19-21; II Cor 6-7; Ps 52-54; Song 4

De 19:14 "You shall not remove your neighbor's landmark, which the men of old have set, in your inheritance which you will inherit in the land that the Lord your God is giving you to possess."

Joel 2:18 "Then the Lord will be zealous for His Land,"

The land He has given us, the land we have gone in to possess, the land we won with our sword which is the Word of God. When I discourage a fellow believer I can take away from his spiritual territory. Causing a brother to stumble in his walk with the Lord is a serious matter.

In the United States there are markers to mark off every mile and a section is a square mile or 640 acres, with a marker at each corner where the vertical and horizontal section lines meet. Can't you see the Israelites placing stones to mark the corners of their land? Moving the stones would be stealing their inheritance.

Day 79 De 22-24; II Cor 8-9; Ps 55-57; Song 5

II Cor 8:1-2 Paul writing to the Church at Corinth is telling of the generosity of the Church of Macedonia. Although in deep poverty, they had put together a large gift to send to Corinth.

II Cor 8:14-15 "but by an equality, that now at this time your abundance may supply their lack, that their abundance also may supply your lack---that there may be equality. As it is written, 'He who gathered much had nothing left over, and he who gathered little had no lack." Ex 16:18

What the Corinthians needed was a spirit of generosity. So each congregation was blessed.

I Cor 12:5-6 "There are differences of ministries, but the same Lord. And there are diversities of activities, but it is the same God who works all in all."

Day 80 De 25-27; II Cor 10-11; Ps 58-60; Song 6

De 25: 5-9 The Law provided for a widow with no children. A woman was considered punished by God if she had no children because there would be no one to take care of her in her old age. She was to be taken by her brother-in-law and the first son would be heir to her dead husband's name and property. If her husband had no brother a near kinsman could redeem her and raise up children for her former husband.

Ruth was a Moabite woman who married a man from Bethlehem and he died without a having a son.

She loved her mother-in-law, Naomi, so much she insisted on returning to Bethlehem with her.

Ruth 1:12-13 Ruth had no guarantee that she would ever have another husband or children, but God rewarded her faith and loyalty. When Ruth went to gather grain for herself and her mother-in-law, she found a good husband and was grandmother of King David. Look for her name in Mt 1:5.

Lev 23:22 "When you reap the harvest of your land, moreover you shall not reap to the very corners of your field nor gather the gleaning of your harvest; you are to leave them for the needy and the alien; I am the Lord your God."

Day 81 De 28-30; II Cor 12-13; Ps 61-63 Song 7

The word Jordan means: to descend, to go downwards; this represents water baptism and baptism represents our willing death to the flesh. The men leaving Egypt were baptized with Moses in the cloud and the sea (I Cor 10:2).

Forty years later when all the men except Joshua and Caleb who were twenty years and older (Numbers 32:11-12) had died in the wilderness, there was need for another baptism. Although they walked through the Red sea on dry land it was a baptism. And when Joshua led them through the Jordan River on dry land it was baptism again.

John the Baptist, baptized for repentance.

Luke 3:16 "John answered and said to them all, 'As for me, I baptize you with water; but One is coming who is mightier than I, and I am not fit to untie the thong of His sandals; He will baptize you with the Holy Spirit and fire."

Day 82 De 31-34; Gal 1-2; Ps 64-66; Song 8

A disagreement came up in the matter of circumcision and following the Law of Moses. Paul informed them that although he was known to be a Greek, Titus was not forced to be circumcised to be accepted by the Jewish believers. Gal 2:3

Rom 7:2 & 4 "For the married woman is bound by law to her husband while he is living; but if her husband dies, she is released from the law concerning the husband. Therefore, my brethren, you also were made to die to the Law through the body of Christ, that you might be joined to another, to Him who was raised from the dead, that we might bear fruit for God."

Gal 3:2-3 "This is the only thing I want to find out from you did you receive the Spirit by the works of the Law, or by hearing with faith? Are you so foolish? Having begun by the Spirit, are you now being perfected by the flesh?"

Josh 1:2 "Moses my servant is dead; now therefore arise, cross this Jordan, you and all this people, to the land which I am giving to them, to the sons of Israel."

Moses is the old leader, representing the old covenant. And Joshua (the Hebrew word meaning savior) is the leader of the new covenant.

Day 83 Josh 1-3; Gal 3-4; Ps 67-69

Josh 1:12 Reuben, Gad and Manasseh were given land on the east side of the Jordan but the mighty men were required to fight for their brethren until all had their own territories. We need mighty men or women to battle for their brethren today until all have come into that place the Lord has prepared for them. This is why the Church is so weak today, those who could be moving mountains are sitting with their feet up watching television or some other time wasting activity, I know I am guilty.

Eph 5:15-16 "Therefore be careful how you walk, not as unwise men, but as wise, making the most of your time, because the days are evil.."

Josh 3:6 "And Joshua spoke to the priests, saying, 'Take up the ark of the covenant and cross over ahead of the people.' So they took up the Ark of the Covenant and went ahead of the people."

We are that royal priesthood who stands between the people and the waters that would otherwise flow over them.

Day 84 Josh 4-6; Gal 5-6; Ps 70-72

Gal 5:22-23 "But the fruit of the spirit is love, joy, peace, patience, kindness, goodness, faithfulness, gentleness, self-control. Against such things there is no law."

Jn 15:5-6 "I am the vine, you are the branches; he who abides in Me, and I in him, he bears much fruit; for apart from Me you can do nothing. If anyone does not abide in Me, he is thrown away as a branch, and dries up; and they gather them, and cast them into the fire, and they are burned."

Why is God so demanding that we produce fruit? It is because the lost are drawn to Him by the display of Spiritual fruit.

Gen 1:29 "Then God said, 'Behold I have given you every plant yielding seed that is on the surface of all the earth, and every tree which has fruit yielding seed; it shall be food for you."

The seed is in the fruit. Yes, the seed is in the fruit! When we produce fruit, the seed is spread around to others.

Ps 126:6 "He who goes to and fro weeping, carrying his bag of seed, shall indeed come again with a shout of joy, bringing his sheaves with him."

Day 85 Josh 7-9; Eph 1-2; Ps 73-75

Josh 7: 11-15 Sin is a reproach to Israel and the sin must be removed.

Because of the perversions of the people that were being driven out by the Lord, different commands came from Him concerning them. Sometimes the people, animals, clothing, everything was to be burned with fire. Some tribes who were defeated, only the young women who were virgins were allowed to live, they would become wives and Israelites. Where demons are worshiped the people are sometimes so polluted with demon possession and disease to the point that they all had to be destroyed. Some people don't understand why innocent children had to die, but if you think how aids can be passed from mother to infant, it is logical.

Ex 15:26 "And said, 'If thou wilt diligently harken to the voice of the Lord thy God and wilt do that which is right in His sight; and wilt give ear to His commandments, and keep all His statutes, I will put none of these diseases upon thee, which I have brought upon the Egyptians; for I am the Lord who healeth thee." (KJV)

Day 86 Josh 10-12; Eph 3-4; Ps 76-78

II Cor 12:4 Paul was taken into Paradise and given unusual knowledge and insight.

Eph 3:9-11 "and to bring to light what is the administration of the mystery, which for ages have been hidden in God, who created all things; in order that the manifold wisdom of God might now be made known through the church to the rulers and the authorities in the heavenly places. This was in accordance with the eternal purpose which He carried out in Christ Jesus our Lord."

Heb 12:1 "Therefore, since we have so great a cloud of witnesses surrounding us, let us also lay aside every encumbrance, and the sin which so easily entangles us, and let us run with endurance the race that is set before us."

We are on display, the Church is a living parable to teach the mysteries of God, which we may have little understanding of ourselves.

Day 87 Josh 13-15; Eph 5-6; Ps 79-81

Ps 79:9&10 "Help us, O God of our salvation, for the glory of Thy name; and deliver us, and forgive our sins, for Thy name's sake. Why should the nations say, 'Where is their God?'"

This seems to be a very self-serving speech. Did they really worry about God's reputation or just want relief for themselves.

God said he would kill the Israelites and make a great nation of Moses but Moses begged for their lives.

Num 14:15-16 "Now if Thou slay this people as one man then the nations who have heard of Thy fame will say, 'Because the Lord could not bring this people into the land which He swore to give them, therefore He killed them in the wilderness."

This was certainly not self-seeking on the part of Moses and I think Asaph was equally unselfish.

Day 88 Josh 16-18; Phil 1-2; Ps 82-84

Israel lost their unity.

Josh 15:63 "Judah could not dislodge the Jebusites, who were living in Jerusalem; to this day the Jebusites live there with the people of Judah."

Josh 16:10 Ephraim did not drive out the Canaanites.

Num 32 Rueben, Gad and Manasseh asked for the land east of the Jordan. Moses commanded that the fighting men go to fight for their brothers until their total victory was complete. The pattern was for all the fighting men to completely destroy the enemy, establish their families and livestock and all the fighting men to go to the next battle. Instead they divided and went to their separate allotment.

They left God's plan of unity to fight alone.

This is a picture of the Church today, separated, weak and unproductive. Pastors have been accused of not feeding the sheep, but stealing the sheep as they try to build numbers in their flock. Other denominations are criticized and looked at with suspicion, it is a sad day, and will stay that way until we learn to look at the main goal of building His Church for His glory.

Day 89 Josh 19-21; Phil 3-4; Ps 85-87

Phil 3:2-3 "Watch out for the dogs, beware of the evil workers, beware of the false circumcision, for we are the true circumcision, who worship in the Spirit of God and glory in Christ Jesus and put no confidence in the flesh,"

There was a running battle between the Jews who held on to the old traditions and Paul as he brought new gentile believers into the Church. Circumcision and baptism are meaningless if it is only in the flesh; am I righteous for life because my parents made a decision to baptize me as an infant, without my consent or understanding, how foolish is that?

Jer 4:4 "Circumcise yourselves to the Lord and remove the foreskins of your heart ... lest My wrath go forth like fire ..."

God demands allegiance of the heart and obedience of the flesh will follow.

The devil wants to divide us into little groups arguing with each other so that we have no power, because then he can defeat us.

Mt 18:19-20 "Again I say to you, that if two of you agree on earth about anything that they may ask, it shall be done for them by My Father who is in heaven. For where two or three have gathered together in My name, there I am in their midst."

(note from the author: the reason I keep repeating the importance of unity is because it is so crucial, without it we are powerless.)

Day 90 Josh 22-24; Col 1-2; Ps 88-90

Josh 24:12-13 "Then I sent the hornet before you and it drove out the two kings of the Amorites from before you, but not by your sword or your bow. And I gave you a land on which you had not labored and cities which you had not built, and you have lived in them, you are eating of vineyards and olive groves which you did not plant."

The Israelites fought and some died and yet they are reminded that there would have been no victory without the Lord.

Ps 124:2&3 "Had it not been the Lord who was on our side, when men rose up against us; then they would have swallowed us alive, when their anger was kindled against us;"

Eph 2:8-9 "For it is by grace you have been saved, through faith; and that not of yourselves, it is the gift of God; not as a result of works, that no one should boast."

Boasting is from pride the sin that condemned Satan.

Day 91 Judges 1-3; Col 3-4; Ps 91-93

After Joshua died the children of Israel asked the Lord "who shall be first to go up for us against the Canaanites to fight against them?" The Lord said Judah would go first, and Judah asked Simeon his brother, who were both sons of Leah, to go with him. Judah means praise and Simeon means obedience. Praise and obedience are powerful forces against the enemy of our soul. When we become Christians we have to fight the habits of the flesh that have been a part of us for so long. Praise takes us into the realm of victory where God is and changes the impossible into the possible and obedience places us in situations where we would be a total fool to go unless the Lord sent us there. Jericho was a strong walled city and yet according to archaeologist the walls fell flat outward, except for a section 54 x 24 feet, Rahab's house.

Josh 6:20 "So the people shouted when the priests blew the trumpets. And it happened when the people heard the sound of the trumpet, and the people shouted with a great shout that the wall fell down flat. Then the people went up into the city, every man straight before him, and they took the city"

Day 92 Judges 4-6; I Thess 1-2; Ps 94-96

Judges 5:31-6:1 "...And the land was undisturbed for forty years. Then the sons of Israel did what was evil in the sight of the Lord; and the Lord gave them into the hands of Midian seven years."

When Israel planted the enemy would come and destroy the crop before it could be harvested. Can you see the enemy waiting to give Israel false hope and swooping in just before the harvest with their herds to devour and trample the fields?

When their time of punishment was finished the Lord called Gideon to fight for Israel. Gideon, hiding in a winepress to save his wheat before it can be taken, is called to defend Israel. Gideon answers that his clan is the weakest and he is the least of his father's house. The humble can be used more quickly than a proud man who will want to use his own strength. Moses had speech problems but God sent him to speak to Pharaoh. Jael was not a soldier, but she put a tent peg through the temple of the mighty king, Sisera.

I Cor 1:27 "but God has chosen the foolish things of the world to shame the wise, and God has chosen the weak things of the world to shame the things which are strong."

The first task for Gideon was to tear down the altar of Baal with its wooden image, and build an altar to the Lord. The men of the city wanted to kill Gideon.

Judges 6:31 "But his father said; will you contend for Baal, or will you deliver him? ... If he is a god let him contend for himself, because someone has torn down his altar"

Day 93 Judges 7-9; I Thess 3-4; Ps 97-99

Judges 7:12 "Now the Midianites, the Amalekites and all the sons of the east were lying in the valley as numerous as locusts; and their camels were without number, as numerous as the sand on the seashore."

Gideon called for men to join him in battle.

Judges 7:2 The Lord said to Gideon, "The people who are with you are too many for Me to give Midian into their hands, lest Israel become boastful, saying My own power has delivered me."

Ex 34:14 "for you shall not worship any other god, for the Lord whose name Jealous, is a jealous God.

"The fearful (22,000) were sent home, and there were 10,000 left, so God set another test and there were 300 left with Gideon. With a trumpet blast and breaking of pitchers the enemy was routed and God was glorified.

Nor are we saved by our own hand, to think so is idolatry.

Eph 2:8-9 "For by grace you have been saved, through faith; and that not of yourselves, it is the gift of God; not as a result of works, so that no one should boast."

Day 94 Judges 10-12; I Thess 5-II Thess 1; Ps 100-102

After the death of Gideon they had peace 45 years then lost it again.

Judges; 10:6-8 "Then the sons of Israel again did evil in the sight of the Lord, served the Baals and the Ashtaroth, the gods of Aram, the gods of Sidon, the gods of Moab, the gods of the sons of Ammon, and the gods of the Philistines; thus they forsook the Lord and did not serve Him. And the anger of the Lord burned against Israel, and He sold them into the hands of the Philistines, and into the hands of the sons of Ammon. And they afflicted and crushed the sons of Israel that year; for eighteen years they afflicted all the sons of Israel who were beyond the Jordan in Gilead in the land of the Amorites."

The great revivals of the past came with much excitement and hunger for the Lord and his Word, the next generation was still doing well, by the third generation their children were becoming mostly lukewarm and ritualistic. It seems it was a pattern for Israel too.

The king of Ammon made war against Israel.

Judges 11:13 "The Ammonites' king replied to the messengers of Jephthah, 'Because Israel took away my land (which was not true), when they came up out of Egypt (300 years before) from the Armon even to Jabbok and to the Jordan; now therefore restore those lands peaceably," (Amplified Bible)

Judges 11:23-24 "Since now the Lord the God of Israel, drove out the Amorites from before His people Israel, are you then to possess it? Do you not possess what Chemosh your god gives you to possess? So whatever the Lord our God has driven out before us, we will possess it.

I think he just said 'my God is bigger than your god.'

The Essential Word

Day 95 Judges 13-15; II Thess 2-3; Ps 103-105

Judges 13:1 "Now the sons of Israel again did evil in the sight of the Lord, so that the Lord gave them into the hands of the Philistines forty years."

The Lord sent the Midianites to punish Israel seven years then delivered them with Gideon. Then He sent the Philistines and Ammonites to punish them for eighteen years and sent Jephthah to free them.

Now they are held captive for forty years and God sends a baby, Samson.

Samson and John the Baptist were Nazarites, born to barren women for a specific purpose. John seems to have lived his life, always guided by the Holy Spirit toward fulfilling God's plan. Samson was a man guided by sexual lust and when he was captured his eyes were put out.

I John 2:16 "For all that is in the world, the lust of the flesh, and the lust of the eyes, and the boastful pride of life, is not from the Father, but is from the world." God had to take his sight before he could be used to his full potential.

In all the striving to get a pay check or to clean the bathroom how many of us are even aware that God has given us a high calling for His use also?

Day 96 Judges 16-18; I Tim 1-2; Ps 106-108

Pharisees wrote laws and regulations supposedly to protect the people from their own ignorance; this is the work of Satan to destroy liberty.

It is a natural tendency of governments to think that they know what is best for us.

Governments need God's covering.

I Tim 2:1-4 "First of all, then I urge that entreaties and prayers, petitions and thanksgivings, be made on behalf of all men, for kings and all who are in authority, in order that we may lead a tranquil and quiet life in all godliness and dignity. This is good and acceptable in the sight of God our Savior, who desires all men to be saved and to come to the knowledge of the truth."

The Israelites were saved over and over when their sin caused God to be angry.

Ps 106:23& 29-31 "Therefore He said that He would destroy them, had not Moses His chosen one stood in the breach, before Him, to turn away His wrath from destroying them. Thus they provoked Him to anger with their deeds, and the plague broke out among them. Then Phinehas stood up and interposed; and so the plague was stayed. And it was reckoned to him for righteousness to all generations forever."

II Cor 5:18-20 "Now all things are from God, who reconciled us to Himself through Christ, and gave us the ministry of reconciliation, namely that God was in Christ reconciling the world to Himself, not counting their trespasses against them, and He has committed to us the word of reconciliation. Therefore, we are ambassadors for Christ, as though God were entreating through us; we beg you on behalf of Christ, be reconciled to God."

Day 97 Judges 19-21; I Tim 3-4; Ps 109-111

Ps 111:9-10 "He sent redemption to His people; He has commanded His covenant forever; holy and awesome is His name. The fear of the Lord is the beginning of wisdom; a good understanding have all those who do His commandments. His praise endures forever."

We hear a lot about love and grace but the fear of the Lord is not preached much today.

Pr 8:13 "The fear of the Lord is to hate evil; pride and arrogance and the evil way and the perverse mouth I hate."

Is 11:1-2 "Then a shoot will spring from the stem of Jesse, and a branch from his roots will bear fruit.

And the Spirit of the Lord will rest on Him, the spirit of wisdom and understanding, the spirit of counsel and strength, the spirit of knowledge and the fear of the Lord. And He will delight in the fear of the Lord," This prophesy of the coming of Jesus says He will fear the Lord.

Fear is another word for respect and awe.

98 Ruth 1-4; I Tim 5-6; Ps 112-114

I Tim 5:3-4 "Honor widows who are widows indeed; but if any widow has children or grandchildren, let them first learn to practice piety in regard to their own family, and to make some return to their parents; for this is acceptable in the sight of God."

Ruth was not obligated under the Law but went because of love for Naomi. She went to fields belonging to strangers to glean. There was personal danger for this woman who had no male relative to protect her but Boaz told his young men not to touch her. By uncovering his feet and lying down, she was asking him to become her husband.

Deut 25:5-10 If a man dies without a son his nearest relative takes her as his wife but the first son will belong to his dead relative. But if he refuses, his shoe is removed in the presence of the elders, which signifies divorce although they never lived together.

The reference to Perez (Ruth 4:18) is because Tamar's second husband refused to give his brother a son and was killed by the Lord, (Gen 38), and she tricked her father-in-law into getting her pregnant.

Day 99 I Sam 1-3; II Tim 1-2; Ps 115-117

Ps 115:4-8 The gods of the gentiles are made by the hands of men and are made with mouths, eyes, ears, noses, hands, which have no use. How could anyone believe a blob of metal or wood could have any power? If I take my coffee cup and set it up on a mantle and pray to it, give thanks to it, ask for favor from it, has it any power? We see this as utter foolishness. But the idols of this world are subtle, based on the devil and his demons that hunger for the worship of men.

Rom 1:18-25 When men reject the truth of God; "their foolish hearts were darkened. Professing to be wise, they became fools, and changed the glory of the incorruptible God into an image made like corruptible man---and birds and four-footed animals and creeping things."

Lucifer, the bright star, became the devil. He longs for the worship of men and angels; he even tried to tempt Jesus to give him worship.

Is 14:12-15 "How you have fallen from heaven, O star of the morning, son of the dawn! You have been cut down to the earth, you who have weakened the nations!

But you said in your heart, I will ascend to heaven; I will raise my throne above the stars of God, and I will sit on the mount of assembly in the recesses of the north. I will ascend above the heights of the clouds; I will make myself like the Most High. Nevertheless you will be thrust down to Sheol, to the recesses of the Pit."

Day 100 I Sam 4-6; II Tim 3-4; Ps 118-120

I Sam 4:1 Israel went out to fight the Philistines and when the battle turned against them they decided to bring the Ark of the Covenant into the battle. The people shouted in triumph when the ark arrived and the Philistines were afraid because "God has come into the camp!" They thought the God who made heaven and earth was in the box. The sons of Eli knew about Him but did not know Him, so they took the ark to force God into battle with them.

Titus 1:16 "They profess to know God, but by their deeds they deny Him, being detestable and disobedient, and worthless for any good deed."

The wife of Phinehas gave birth and named the child Ichabod, saying, that the glory had departed from Israel. The power of God was gone long before this but they had not seen it leave. Just as Samson said,

Judges 16:20 "I will go out as at other times, and shake myself free!' But he did not know that the Lord had departed from him."

To have the power of God, we have to stay close to Him. He does not follow us, we have to follow Him. Over and over Jesus said, "Follow Me." The glory of the Lord is found in Jesus.

Day 101 I Sam 7-9; Titus 1-2; Ps 121-123

I Sam 8:5 The elders came to Samuel and said, "Behold, you have grown old, and your sons do not walk in your ways. Now appoint a king for us to judge us like all the nations." Samuel warned them that they were rejecting God and a king would take a tenth of their produce and their sons and daughters to be his servants but the elders would not listen. The Lord chose Saul, of the tribe of Benjamin.

I Sam 9:21 "Saul answered and said, 'Am I not a Benjamite, of the smallest of the tribes of Israel,"

The tribe of Benjamin in Numbers 1:37, had 35,400 men 20 years and older able to fight.

Judges 19:22-26. Because they practiced sodomy a group of them demanded a visitor be given to them for sexual use. Instead the man's concubine was given to them and they raped her till she died. The other tribes went to kill all of the Benjamites and fought until only 600 men escaped. Years later God chose one from the smallest and least respected tribe to rule over Israel. They should have seen God's contempt for their plan but went blindly into bondage to a king.

Jer 6:16 "Thus says the Lord, 'Stand by the ways and see and ask for the ancient paths, where the good way is, and walk in it; and you shall find rest for your souls, but they said 'We will not walk in it."

Day 102 I Sam 10-12; Titus 3-Philem 1; Ps 124-126

Ps 126:5-6 "Those who sow in tears shall reap with joyful shouting. He who goes to and fro weeping and carrying his bag of seed, shall indeed come again with a shout of joy bringing his sheaves with him."

When you pray desperate prayers for a loved one to be saved, don't be surprised if things get much worse before they get better. Don't interfere with God's judgment on them. If it means going bankrupt or to prison, say, "Thank you Lord for moving in their life!" When they have a crisis, they may become willing to see their need.

When things are not going well, people may become more approachable and re-examine their life and have a crack in their arrogant veneer.

IICor 4:3-4 "And even if our gospel is veiled, it is veiled to those who are perishing. In whose case the god of this world has blinded the minds of the unbelieving, that they might not see the light of the gospel of the glory of Christ who is the image of God."

When you pray, agree with the scriptures. Rom 1:21 God said "Let there be light" and we can ask Him to send His light into their dark minds. Rom 1:21 The devil has blinded, but God wants to give them sight.

Day 103 I Sam 13-15; Heb 1-2; Ps 127-129

James 1:3 "Knowing that the testing of your faith produces endurance."

I pray and I wait, I pray some more and wait, I'm getting old, I don't want patience, I want results.

Ps 37:8-10 "...Do not fret, it only leads to evildoing. For evildoers shall be cut off, but those who wait for the Lord, they shall inherit the land. Yet a little while and the wicked will be no more;"

I Sam 13 War is eminent, the enemy is strong, 30,000 chariots, 6,000 horsemen, and innumerable soldiers. Still Saul waits 7 days for Samuel. Samuel said he would be there in 7 days, so where is he? The army of Saul keeps shrinking as people sneak away in the night to go home. So, Saul presented the burnt offering to the Lord himself and then Samuel shows up.

I Sam 15:22-23 "And Samuel said, "Has the Lord as much delight in burnt offerings and sacrifices as in obeying the voice of the Lord? Behold, to obey is better than sacrifice; and to heed than the fat of rams. For rebelling is as the sin of divination, and insubordination is as iniquity and idolatry. Because you have rejected the word of the Lord, He has rejected you from being king."

This sounds pretty harsh but God doesn't talk just to hear His own voice. What if Gideon rejected the idea of telling almost all the troops to go home; he would not have had success. (From Day 93)

Day 104 I Sam 16-18; Heb 3-4; Ps 130-132

Samuel had come to love Saul, and grieved because the Lord had rejected him. Saul was a tall handsome man and had a kingly bearing. The Lord sent Samuel to the house of Jesse, and the oldest son looked good to Samuel.

I Sam 16:7 "But the Lord said to Samuel, 'Do not look at his appearance or at the height of his stature, because I have rejected him; for God sees not as man sees, for man looks at the outward appearance, but the Lord looks at the heart."

David had a shepherd's heart, a caregiver's heart, serving and protecting as he worshiped the Lord. As a young man he was skillful with the harp (I Sam 16:16) which soothed Saul's tormented soul. Many of the songs of worship that we sing today were sung and written by David. God does not need our worship; we have the need to worship. Worship draws us into the very heart of God. David could sing, Ps 23:1 "The Lord is my shepherd, I shall not want."

David could look at Goliath and say; "Your servant has killed both lion and bear; and this uncircumcised Philistine will be like one of them, since he has taunted the armies of the living God." Goliath had insulted the God of Israel. Like God, David was not moved by the outward appearance.

Day 105 I Sam 19-21; Heb 5-6; Ps 133-135

Ps 133:1 "Behold, how good and how pleasant it is for brothers to dwell together in unity! It is like the precious oil upon the head, coming down on the beard, even Aaron's beard, coming down upon the edge of his robes."

The anointing oil represents the Holy Spirit on our lives.

Is 10:27 "So it will be in that day, that his burden will be removed from your shoulders and his yoke from your neck, and the yoke will be broken because of fatness (the anointing oil)."

Mt 11:28-30 "Come to Me, all you who are weary and heavy laden, and I will give you rest. Take My yoke upon you and learn of Me, for I am gentle and humble in heart, and you shall find rest for your souls, for My yoke is easy and My burden is light."

Paul was very upset when the Galatians were trying to obey the Law and live in grace.

Gal 5:1 "It was for freedom that Christ set us free; therefore keep standing firm and do not be subject again to a yoke of slavery."

Day 106 I Sam 22-24; Heb 7-8; Ps 136-138; Pr 1

Saul is obsessed with killing David. He knows David has been anointed by Samuel to be king. He blames David instead of his own failure. He actually thinks that if he can get David out of the picture he can keep his crown. He was not fighting David, he was fighting God. When David could have killed Saul he would not.

I Sam 24:13 "As the proverb of the ancients says, 'Out of the wicked comes forth wickedness..'"

Mt 7:16-17 "You will know them by their fruits. Grapes are not gathered from thorn bushes, nor figs from thistles, are they?"

Although Saul had real affection for David, he tried to destroy him for selfish ambition.

Rom 12:19-21 "Never take your own revenge, beloved, but leave room for the wrath of God, for it is written, 'Vengeance is mine, I will repay,' says the Lord. But if your enemy is hungry, feed him, and if he is thirsty, give him a drink; for in so doing you will heap burning coals upon his head. Do not be overcome by evil, but overcome evil with good." If you forgive them, God will forgive them.

Day 107 I Sam 25-28; Heb 9-10; Ps 139-141; Pr 2

Nabal (I Sam25:2 & 8) was a very rich man and his shepherds and herds had been protected by David. David had a right to expect a good reply.

De 15:7-8 "If there is a poor man with you, one of your brothers, in any of your towns in your land which the Lord your God is giving you, you shall not harden your heart, nor close your hand from your poor brother, but you shall freely open your hand to him and shall generously lend him sufficient for his need in whatever he lacks."

This is not to say David would owe a debt to Nabal, David's debt would be to the Lord because the Lord will repay.

Lev 19:18 "You shall not take vengeance, nor bear any grudge against the sons of your people, but you shall love your neighbor as yourself, I am the Lord."

Abigail kept David from taking vengeance and shedding innocent blood by her godly behavior. Nabal had what seems to be a stroke and had time to repent (we hope he did) in the ten days before God took his life.

Day 108 I Sam 29-31; Heb 11-12; Ps 142-144; Pr 3

Hebrews 12:12 "Therefore strengthen the hands that are weak and the knees that are feeble," (Read Job 4:3-4)

Ex 17:8-13 Amalek came to attack and Moses stood on top of a hill with hands held up with the rod of God. While his hands were up Israel was winning and when his arms got tired and started to hang down they would lose. But Moses had help from Aaron and Hur who supported his arms. We all need support at times and need brothers and sisters to help. Maybe its prayer (prayer is always the first thing) or a word of encouragement; mowing a lawn; bringing in meals; driving them somewhere. Whatever the need we should always be ready and willing. This is an admonition to gather our own strength and to help those who cannot help themselves.

Is 35:3-6 "Encourage the exhausted, and strengthen the feeble. Say to those with anxious heart, take courage, fear not. Behold, your God will come with vengeance; the recompense of God will come, but He will save you. Then the eyes of the blind will be opened and, and the ears of the deaf will be unstopped. Then the lame will leap like a deer, and the tongue of the dumb will shout for joy."

Day 109 II Sam 1-3; Heb 13-James 1; Ps 145-147; Pr 4

James 1:2 "Consider it all joy, my brethren, when you encounter various trials, knowing that the testing of your faith produces endurance."

Heb 13:15 "Through Him then, let us continually offer up a sacrifice of praise to God, that is, the fruit of our lips, that give thanks to His name."

Build a habit of praise, it will serve you well all of your life. Sometimes praise comes easy and sometimes you have to bring the sacrifice, not of the blood of sheep or goats, but a costly sacrifice, all the same.

Ex 30:15 As the Lord says: "The rich shall not pay more and the poor shall not pay less…."

One sacrifice paid for our salvation to bring us into fellowship with our Father. There is only one way, His way through the sacrifice of Jesus and our sacrifice is so much easier, all he asks for is a sacrifice of Praise.

Day 110 II Sam 4-6; James 2-3; Ps 148-150; Pr 5

Ps 149:1-3 "Praise the Lord! Sing to the Lord a new song, and His praise in the congregation of the godly ones. Let Israel be glad in his maker; let the sons of Zion rejoice in their King. Let them praise His name with dancing; let them sing praises to Him with the timbrel and lyre. For the Lord takes pleasure in His people; He will beautify the afflicted ones with salvation."

A new song is when you open your mouth and allow Him to give you words, words you have never heard, praise just comes out.

Ps 150:2-6 "Praise Him for His mighty deeds; praise Him according His excellent greatness! Praise Him with the trumpet sound; praise Him; praise Him with the harp and lyre. Praise Him with timbrel and dancing; praise Him with stringed instruments and pipe. Praise Him with loud cymbals; praise Him with resounding cymbals! Let everything that has breath praise the Lord. Praise the Lord!"

David had extreme joy to bring the ark of God into the City of David. As he danced with leaping and whirling, (II Sam 6:16) Michal saw and despised him. She was Saul's daughter and it offended her dignity. She did not know God nor understand worship.

Day 111 II Sam 7-9; James 4-5; Ps 1-3; Pr 6

Adam and Eve had their nakedness covered with the skin of at least one animal. In the tabernacle in the wilderness the people had their sin covered by the blood of animals. Jesus did more than cover our sins, He blotted them out, totally removed them. We cannot pay the price of sin in others with our death, but we still have responsibility to administer grace.

James 5:19-20 "My brethren, if anyone among you strays from the truth, and one turns him back, let him know that he who turns a sinner from the error of his way will save a soul from death and will cover a multitude of sins."

Pr 10:12 "Hatred stirs up strife, but love covers all transgressions."

I Peter 4:8 "Above all keep fervent in your love for one another, because love covers a multitude of sins."

David's love for Jonathon made him save Mephibosheth and make sure he did not suffer want. Eating at the kings table was more than feeding him, it was showing him extreme honor. Eating at the king's table was showing him extreme honor not necessarily eating together but that the king would furnish all his food.

Day 112 II Sam 10-12; I Pet 1-2; Ps 4-6; Pr 7

David was a godly man who loved the Lord and shows how to worship with abandon. But one evening he was drawn by the lust of the eye and reveals to us we can be caught if we are careless.

If Bathsheba didn't intend to be seen wouldn't she have screened herself from view? Rooftop bathing was common; rain water was collected and warmed by the sun. Did she have any choice to say yes or no when the king sent for her? There is no way to know what Bathsheba wanted. When she became pregnant, David tried to keep their sin hidden. Her husband Uriah was brought back from the war zone. When he refused to have pleasure with his wife while men were still on the battlefield, David had him killed. Nathan, the prophet came to him with a little parable to show David the error of his ways. He repented at once.

II Sam 12:13-14 "Then David said to Nathan, 'I have sinned against the Lord.' and Nathan said to David, "The Lord also has taken away your sin; you shall not die. However, because by this deed you have given occasion to the enemies of the Lord to blaspheme, the child also that is born to you shall surely die,"

David fasted and pleaded with the Lord, but the child died. Then David got up, cleaned himself and went to the house of the Lord and worshiped; and he sang to the Lord Psalm 51.

And I thank God there were scribes there to record the song.

Day 113 II Sam 13-16; I Pet 3-4; Ps 7-9; Pr 8

I Peter 3:12 "For the eyes of the Lord are upon the righteous, and His ears attend to their prayer; but the face of the Lord is against those who do evil."

Is 49:24-25 "Shall the prey be taken from the mighty, or the lawful captive delivered? But thus saith the Lord, 'Even the captives of the mighty shall be taken away, and the prey of the terrible shall be delivered: for I will contend with him that contendeth with thee, and I will save thy children.'"

Leaders rise up and think they are very great, and make slaves of those who are helpless but their end is always the same.

Gal 6:7 "Do not be deceived, God is not mocked; for whatever a man sows, this he will also reap."

Their slavery may not be visible on this earth but it is now and inevitable.

Day 114 II Sam 17-19; I Pet 5- II Pet 1; Ps 10-12; Pr:9

I Pet 5:5-6 "You younger men, likewise, be subject to your elders; and all of you, clothe yourselves with humility toward one another, for God is opposed to the proud, but gives grace to the humble. Humble yourselves therefore under the mighty hand of God, that He may exalt you at the proper time.

Absalom became proud and thought he deserved to be king. He raised an army to fight against his own father. David loved Absalom and wanted to protect him from being killed in battle. But, Joab was fighting to save David's life and kingdom. When the opportunity came to end the war, he killed Absalom himself. Joab had to reprimand David when he grieved loudly for Absalom because David cared more for the death of Absalom than for the men who had fought and died for him.

When fighting for the salvation of our children or others, the battle can be long and discouraging but in the end we can win.

Gal 6:9 "And let us not lose heart in doing good, for in due time we shall reap if we do not grow weary."

Day 115 II Sam 20-22; II Pet 2-3; Ps 13-15; Pr 10

II Sam 21 When David asked the Lord why there was three years of famine in the land, God told him it was because Saul had tried to destroy the Gibeonites. (Josh 9:16 The Gibeonites tricked Joshua into a peace treaty).

The Gibeonites demanded seven sons of Saul be given to them to be put to death. David spared the sons of Jonathon, but gave two sons of Saul by his wife Rizpah and five sons of Michal, after she had been taken from David and given to her second husband. I Sam 25:44. The shedding of the Gibeonite's innocent blood defiled the land and had to be redeemed.

Num 35:33 "So you shall not pollute the land in which you are; for blood pollutes the land and no expiation can be made for the land for the blood that is shed on it, except by the blood of him who shed it."

Blood has a voice that God can hear. When Cain killed Abel, God came to ask about Abel and Cain pretended ignorance.

Gen 4:10 "...The voice of your brother's blood is crying out to Me from the ground."

How great must the cry be from the United States where so much innocent blood has been shed? We, the church, need to heal our land.

II Chr 7:14 "If My people which are called by My name, shall humble themselves, and pray, and seek My face, and turn from their wicked ways; then I will hear from heaven, and will forgive their sin and heal their land." (KJV)

Day 116 II Sam 23- I K 1; I John 1-2; Ps 16-18; Pr 11

Pr 11:2 "When pride comes, then comes dishonor; but with the humble is wisdom."

I Kings 1:5 "Then Adonijah the son of Hagith exalted himself, saying, 'I will be king'; so prepared for himself chariots and horsemen, and fifty men to run before him."

The name Adonijah means 'my Lord is Jehovah and Absalom means 'father of peace.' They fell way short of living up to their names.

Absalom saw himself as king and tried to take the throne while David was still strong. Adonijah saw that David was old and frail and moved to be king. They had traits more like Saul than their father, David. Nathan the prophet came to Bathsheba and between them they caused Solomon to be made king before war could break out as it had with Absalom. Solomon allowed Adonijah to go home in peace. But, Adonijah made a mistake when he would not be content to live in peace. He lost his life when he asked for Abishag to be his wife. Abishag was the young woman brought in to comfort and warm David when he was dying and was considered a wife, although David did not consummate the union.

Day 117 I K 2-4; I John 3-4; Ps 19-21; Pr 12

I John 4:7-8 "Beloved, let us love one another, for love is from God; and everyone who loves is born of God and knows God. The one who does not love does not know God, for God is love"

II John 3:18 "My little children, let us not love in word or in tongue, but in deed and in truth."

The Lord does not want to see a pious shell or a holy veneer. He looks at the heart. Jesus had harsh words for the outward pretense and public fastings.

Mt 23:27 "Woe to you scribes and Pharisees, hypocrites! For you are like whitewashed tombs which appear beautiful, but inside they are full of dead men's bones and all uncleanness."

Is 58:6-7 "Is this not the fast which I have chosen; to loose the bonds of wickedness, to undo the bands of the yoke, to let the oppressed go free, and that you break every yoke? Is it not to divide your bread with the hungry, and bring the homeless poor into the house; when you see the naked, to cover him; and not to hide yourself from your own flesh?"

It makes me shiver to know how far I fall short in what I should be doing.

Day118 I K 5-8; I John 5-II Jn 1; Ps 22-24; Pr 13

I K 8:33-34 "When Thy people Israel are defeated before an enemy because they have sinned against Thee, and when they turn back to Thee and confess Thy name, and pray and make supplication to Thee in this house, then hear Thou in heaven, and forgive the sin of Thy people Israel, and bring them back to the land which Thou didst give to their fathers."

I Cor 3:16 "Do you not know that you are the temple of God and that the Spirit of God dwells in you?"

We know that we are the temple, and wherever we are the Holy Spirit is there. We don't have to travel to a special place to get God's ear. I enjoy church services, I love the music, but I don't have to wait a single minute to worship. Worship takes place in the temple. The 'Land' is the peace we find in worship and obedience. As Israel came into their inheritance, they would sin and repent, sin and repent, sin and repent.

The Essential Word ⅠⅠⅠⅠ 99

Are we so different from them, it is easy to judge because we are so good at hiding our shortcomings.

Day 119 I K 9-11; III John –Jude; Ps 25-27; Pr 14

Jude 1:12 "These men are those who are hidden reefs in your love feasts when they feast with you without fear, caring for themselves; clouds without water carried along by winds; autumn trees without fruit, doubly dead uprooted;"

There are people who make themselves great through the power of their oratory, but their heart is not with the Lord. When we follow men instead of God there will be divisions and the separating of the body of Christ.

Rom 16:17 "Now I urge you, brethren, keep your eye on those who cause dissensions and hindrances contrary to the teaching which you learned and turn away from them."

The church lacks strength because our doctrines are more important to us than gathering ourselves together for building the kingdom of the Lord. On day 253, the name Gad means gathering together in a troop.

Acts 2:42 "And they were continually devoting themselves to the apostles' teaching and to fellowship, the breaking of bread and to prayer."

Doctrine is very important but we will win more with love than criticism.

Day 120 I K 12-14; Rev 1-2; Ps 28-30; Pr 15

I K 11:28-31 Solomon loved many women and made places of worship for their gods and enslaved the people to labor for him and appointed Jeroboam over all the labor force of the house of Joseph. The Prophet, Ahijah took his garment and tore it into 12 pieces and told Jeroboam to take 10 pieces to represent the 10 tribes where he would be king.

I K 12:1 & 3-4 Solomon's son, Rehoboam was made king. "…. Jeroboam and all the assembly came to Rehoboam, saying, 'Your father made our yoke hard; therefore lighten the hard service of your father, and his heavy yoke which he put on us, and we will serve you." After getting wise council of old men which he rejected, Rehoboam asked advice of his young men.

I K 12:14 "and he spoke to them according to the advice of the young men, saying, 'My father made your yoke heavy, but I will add to your yoke; my father disciplined you with whips, but I will discipline you with scorpions."

I K 12:18-19 "Then King Rehoboam sent Adoram, who was over the forced labor, and all Israel stoned him to death. So Israel has been in rebellion against the house of David to this day."

Day 121 I K 15-17; Rev 3-4; Ps 31-33; Pr 16

I K 15:11 & 14 "and Asa did what was right in the sight of the Lord like David his father. But the high places were not taken away; nevertheless the heart of Asa was wholly devoted to the Lord all his days."

The high places were places dedicated to the worship of demons and caused there to be wars and turmoil through the many years of the kings. Elijah came into prominence and turned many back to the Lord through the miracles God gave him. Elijah's calling is not that different than our calling. We are called to turn people to repentance and relationship with Jesus. The high places of the heart need to be torn down.

Judges 6:27 Gideon had to tear down the altar of worship built by his father and cut down the grove; he went by night because he feared his father and the men of the city.

To tear down an altar in a person's life, you may have to be confrontational and other times you have to be more stealthy. Follow God's leading and always pray before you make any bad moves, while, during and after you work with them.

Day 122 I K 18-21; Rev 5-6; Ps 34-36; Pr 17

I K 19:19 Elijah was told by the Lord that Elisha was chosen to be prophet after him. He found Elisha plowing with twelve yoke of oxen.

A yoke is a wooden beam shaped to make two oxen pull together equally. Oxen are castrated as calves to become large and strong whose whole purpose is to pull heavy loads. The oxen had to be well trained for twenty-four to pull straight and steady.

Mt 11:28-30 Jesus said, "Come to Me, all you who labor and are heavy laden, and I will give you rest, take My yoke upon you and learn from Me, for I am gentle and humble in heart, and you shall find rest for your souls, for My yoke is easy and My burden is light."

II Cor 6:14 "Do not be bound together with unbelievers; for what partnership have righteousness and lawlessness, or what fellowship has light with darkness?"

The yoke of sin is very heavy and an unbeliever and a believer will never be able to pull toward the same goal.

Mt 18:19 "Again I say to you that if two of you agree on earth about anything that they ask, it shall be done for them by My Father in heaven."

Can you imagine what 24 Christians pulling together could accomplish?

Day 123 I K 22- II K 2; Rev 7-8; Ps 37-39; Pr 18

I K 22 The prophet Micaiah told Ahab that he would not come back from battle with Syria and live. But Ahab king of Israel enticed Jehoshaphat the king of Judah to join him in battle against Syria.

I K 22:30 "And the king of Israel said to Jehoshaphat, 'I will disguise myself and go into battle; but you put on your robes."

Ahab didn't care that Jehoshaphat would be a target for the Syrians and probably get killed and Jehoshaphat seemed to be a little dim-witted.

So the king of Israel disguised himself and went into battle. But, God's plans will not be undone by clothing or any other disguise.

V. 34 "Now a certain man drew a bow at random, and struck the king of Israel between the joints of his armor".

When Ahab's blood was washed out of the chariot the dogs licked it up, fulfilling the prophecy given by Elijah;

I K 21:19 "…Thus says the Lord: 'In the place where dogs licked up the blood of Naboth, the dogs shall lick your blood, even yours"

Day 124 II K 3-5; Rev 9-10; Ps 40-42; Pr 19

II K 5:16-27 The gifts of God are not to be bought or sold. Elisha refused gifts for the healing of Naaman. But, greed rose up in Elisha's servant Gehazi and he ran after the Syrian to get some of the riches that had been offered to Elisha. When Elisha confronted him, Gehazi became white with leprosy.

Acts 8:18-21 "Now when Simon saw that the Spirit was bestowed through the laying on of the apostles' hands, he offered them money, saying, 'Give this authority to me as well so that everyone on whom I lay my hands may receive the Holy Spirit.' But Peter said to him, 'May your silver perish with you, because you thought you could obtain the gift of God with money!"

How we use money reveals our heart to God and anyone who is watching, we don't want God to be reviled because of our actions.

Day 125 II K 6-8; Rev 11-12; Ps 43-45; Pr 20

II K 6 The king of Syria went to war against Israel and laid ambushes for the king of Israel, Elisha warned Israel not to go to the places of ambush. The king of Syria thought there was a spy in his camp. A servant told him that the prophet of Israel was warning their king, so he sent a great army to bring Elisha back to him. When the young servant of Elisha got up in the morning and saw the city surrounded he was terrified. Elisha asked the Lord to open the young man's eyes and he saw the mountains around them filled with fiery horses and chariots. Elisha prayed for the army to be made blind and then led them to Samaria where they made peace.

Some people can see angels today. I think I saw an angel once, he looked like a man and I was never sure, but I know I felt the hands of an angel at another time. I had just come into a deeper relation with the Lord than ever before and I had a hunger for the Bible. Every time I would try to read I got so sleepy I couldn't hold my eyes open. I saw it for the attack of the devil it was, but couldn't stay awake. I lay down on the couch and closed my eyes. Suddenly I felt hands firmly on both sides just above the waist.

I was lying on my side facing the room so the hands had to come through the couch. When I turned over to see who was there, there was no one visible. Well, I was wide awake then! The heavy drowsiness that hit me every time I picked up my Bible didn't come back.

Heb 1:14 "Are they not all ministering spirits sent forth to minister for those who will inherit salvation?" Maybe we should look for more and expect more.

Day 126 II K 9-11; Rev 13-14; Ps 46-48; Pr 21

I K 21 Naboth had a vineyard and as soon as Ahab looked at it he wanted to turn it into an herb garden for himself. Naboth refused to sell his inheritance that had been allotted to his ancestor when they first came out of the wilderness with Joshua. Jezebel thought any whim she or her husband had should be granted so she had Naboth and his sons killed.

Luke 6:45 "A good man out of the good treasure of his heart brings forth good; and an evil man out of the evil treasure of his heart brings forth evil. For out of the abundance of the heart his mouth speaks."

Sin is conceived in the mind, our feet take us to the place and our hands finish the deed.

I K 9:35 When men came to bury Jezebel, nothing was found but her skull, her feet and the palms of her hands. She had been eaten by dogs in the field that had been stolen from Naboth.

II K 11:1 And when Athaliah the mother of Ahaziah saw that her son was dead she arose and destroyed all the royal heirs, her own grandchildren. But Johosheba, sister of Ahaziah took Joash the son of Ahaziah, and hid him. Jehoiada the priest hid him in the temple for 6 years and made a covenant with the child king to destroy the worship of Baal.

These two evil and power mad women both came to a violent death.

Day 127 II K 12-14; Rev 15-16; Ps 49-51; Pr 22

In Rev 8 there are trumpets and in chapter 16 there are vials of wrath poured out on the earth. We can't ignore the similarities with the plagues of Egypt when Moses went to bring Israel out of bondage.

Water is turned to blood, the sun is darkened, hail weighing a talent which is about 75 pounds. It is a time of chaos and horrible suffering, but the Lord is with us. The saints of the early church were tortured, imprisoned, beheaded and many other things that the minds of evil men can imagine. As Stephen was stoned he saw the Lord. We have to overcome the enemy and our own weakness to be saved. Loving the Lord is easy in good times but sometimes we have to grit our teeth and hold on through suffering. The earth will not be here forever.

Is 24:19-20 "The earth is broken asunder, the earth is split through, the earth is shaken violently, the earth reels to and fro like a drunkard, and it totters like a shack, for its transgression is heavy upon it, and it will fall, never to rise again."

Day 128 II K 15-17; Rev 17-18; Ps 52-54; Pr 23

Depend on the Lord, there is no one or no thing that can save or protect you except Him.

Ps 52:1 & 7-9 "Why do you boast in evil, O mighty man? The lovingkindness of God endures all day long. Behold, the man who would not make God his refuge, but trusted in the abundance of his riches, and was strong in his evil desire. But as for me, I am like a green olive tree in the house of God; I trust in the lovingkindness of God forever and ever. I will give Thee thanks forever, because Thou hast done it. And I will wait on Thy name, for it is good in the presence of Thy godly ones."

Ps 20:7 "Some boast in chariots, and some in horses; but we boast in the name of the Lord our God."

We trust our spouse, our family or even our house to protect us in the storms of life, but they will fail us because only the Lord has the power and He never wants anything but what is best for us. He is faithful to provide our needs but that doesn't mean we always get what we want like spoiled children.

Pr 3:5-6 "Trust in the Lord with all your heart, and do not lean on your own understanding; in all your ways acknowledge Him, and He will make your paths straight."

Day 129 II K 18-20; Rev 19-20; Ps 55-57; Pr 24

II K 18:13 Sennacherib, king of Assyria after sweeping conquests all around, came against Judah. First Hezekiah stripped the house of the Lord of gold and silver to bribe him to leave Judah alone. Then the threat came from Sennacherib that the gods of the other nations had not been able to stop him and the God of Judah would also fail. Look at the similarity with Goliath who trusted in his own size and strength and he dared to reproach the living God also. Hezekiah sent a messenger to the prophet Isaiah and received an answer that they would not be attacked and the Lord also had a word for Sennacherib.

II K 19:27-28 "But I know your going out and coming in, and your rage against Me and ….I will put My hook in your nose and My bridle in your lips; and I will turn you back by the way which you came." In one night an angel came from the Lord and killed 185,000 of his army and Sennacherib turned and went home.

Trouble then and now all have the same answer, humble yourself and pray.

Day 130 II K 21-23; Rev 21-22; Ps 58-60; Pr 25

Josiah was a good king and wanted to do the right thing. He began to repair the house of the Lord.

When they began the repairs the book of the Law was found. When he realized how they had sinned he tore his clothes and made a covenant with the Lord to make many changes. He brought articles that were made for Baal, Ashtoreth and for all the hosts of heaven out of the temple and burned them. He commanded the people to keep the Passover again.

II K 23:25 "And before him there was no king like him, who turned to the Lord with all his heart, with all his soul, and with all his might, according to all the Law of Moses; nor did any like him arise after him."

We have the helper, the Holy Spirit in us to guide us from within, so what Josiah accomplished was extremely great.

De 10:12-13 "And now, Israel, what does the Lord your God require from you, but to fear the Lord your God, to walk in all His ways and love Him, and to serve the Lord your God with all your heart and with all your soul, and to keep the Lord's commandments and His statutes which I am commanding you today for you good."

Josiah did what he could to bring back true worship.

Day 131 II K 24- I Chr 1; Mt 1-2; Ps 61-63; Pr 26

Mt 1 This list of men in the genealogy goes from Abraham to Jesus, but includes four women.

Gen 38:6-30 Tamar was a young woman who was married to Er, a wicked man and God killed him. Then she was married to his brother, Onan according to the Law. (De 25:5-9) Onan was also wicked for when it came time for him to produce a son for his brother, he purposely spilled his seed on the ground and God killed him. Judah her father-in-law blamed her for the death of his sons and would not give her his third son. After she realized the way it was; she dressed as a harlot and got pregnant by her father-in-law.

Josh 2:1-3 Rahab was a harlot In Jericho. She hid the Hebrew spies from the men of the town

Heb 11:31 "By faith Rahab the harlot did not perish along with those who were disobedient, after she had welcomed the spies in peace."

Josh 2:9 "and she said to the men, 'I know that the Lord has given you the land, that the terror of you has fallen on us,"

She and her family lived and she married one the spies then became the mother of Boaz and entered the line of promise.

Ruth was of Moab and her husband died without children. Refusing to allow her mother-in-law to go back to Bethlehem without her, she also moved into the ancestry of Jesus. She married Boaz who was a close relative of her husband's family. One man was closer and had the right to claim Ruth as his wife, but he chose not to claim his right.

II Sam 11:1-2 Bathsheba was the wife of Uriah. David saw her bathing and sent a servant to fetch her.

She became his wife and gave birth to Solomon.

All these women were not in a position to be in the genealogy naturally, but God placed them there.

Day 132 I Chr 2-4; Mt 3-4; Ps 64-66; Pr 27

Luke 1:15 An angel appeared to Zacharias to tell him a son would be born to him that would be filled with the Holy Spirit from the womb. When Mary was with child she went to see Elizabeth.

Luke1:41-44 "And it came about that when Elizabeth heard Mary's greeting the baby leaped in her womb; and Elizabeth was filled with the Holy Spirit. And she cried out with a loud voice, and said, 'Blessed among women are you, and blessed is the fruit of your womb! And how has it happened to me, that the mother of my Lord should come to me? For behold, when the sound of your greeting reached my ears, the baby leaped in my womb for joy,"

John the Baptist came preaching repentance. When Pharisees and Sadducees came to be baptized, John called them a "Brood of vipers".

Mt 3:13 Then Jesus came to be baptized by him. John recognized by the Spirit the Pharisees and Sadducees and Jesus. The religious leaders had not come because of repentance but to follow the crowd, to be seen and find out who John was. We are not to judge and condemn, that which belongs to God, but we should have discernment and sometimes the Lord will use you to speak words of correction, but always in love.

Day 133 I Chr 5-7; Mt 5-6; Ps 67-69; Pr 28

Mt 5:4 "Blessed are those who mourn, for they shall be comforted."

What do we mourn for? Do we mourn for the godly parent or grandparent that has gone home to Jesus? We should be thanking God every day that they are beyond the pain of arthritis, cancer or other ailments of the aged. We can miss their presence without having a mourning spirit.

Ps 30:11 "Thou hast turned for me my mourning into dancing; Thou hast loosed my sackcloth and girded me with gladness."

Is 61:3 "To grant (consolation and joy) to those who mourn in Zion, to give them an ornament---a garland or diadem---of beauty instead of ashes, the oil of joy for mourning, the garment (expressive) of praise instead of a heavy, burdened and failing spirit; that they may be called oaks of righteousness (lofty, strong and magnificent, distinguished for uprightness, justice and right standing with God), the planting of the Lord, that He may be glorified." (Amplified Bible)

I Thess 4:13 "But we do not want you to be uninformed, brethren, about those who are asleep, that you may not grieve, as do the rest who have no hope."

We are not like the heathen; we know where we are heading. Mourn for the lost and cry out to God while there is still time. I mourn for my grandchildren who have heard the gospel all their lives but have no time for the Lord. And yet, I have hope and the assurance that God is faithful. Prayer is the most overlooked but most powerful work we can perform.

Day 134 I Chr 8-10; Mt 7-8; Ps 70-72; Pr 29

Mt 7:7 & 11 "Ask, and it shall be given to you; seek, and you shall find; knock, and it shall be opened to you. If you then, being evil, know how to give good gifts to your children, how much more shall your Father who is in heaven give what is good to those who ask Him!"

We love our children and want to give them things that will make them happy, but if we give them everything they want they will not be very healthy. He wants us to work with Him. We cannot expect Him to work with us, when we are not in His will.

James 4:3 "You ask and do not receive because you ask with wrong motives, that you may spend it on your pleasures."

A few years back the prosperity teaching was everywhere. Ask and receive sounded so good. But, if your mind is on earthly things, who is answering your prayer; our Father in heaven or the god of this world?

It is time to grow up and put childish things behind us, it is time to seek His will and not ours.

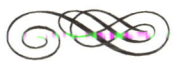

Day 135 I Chr 11-13; Mt 9-10; Ps 73-75; Pr 30

Mt 9:16 "No one puts a patch of unshrunk cloth on an old garment; for the patch pulls away from the garment, and a worse tear results."

We are sinners and when we come to know Jesus we are made new, but Jesus is not a patch on our old life. He wants to transform us. He is patient to allow us to start small. As a baby we start with faltering steps long before we can walk with confidence. That is only the beginning of our new life.

Job 8:7 "Though thy beginning was small, yet thy latter end should greatly increase." (KJV)

Heb 12:1-2 "Therefore since we have so great a cloud of witnesses surrounding us, let us also lay aside every encumbrance; and the sin which so easily entangles us, and let us run with endurance the race that is set before us, fixing our eyes on Jesus, who for the joy set before Him endured the cross."

Day 136 I Chr 14-16; Mt 11-12; Ps 76-78; Pr 31

I Chr 14:9-10 & 13-15 "Now the Philistines had come and made a raid in the valley of Rephaim. And David inquired of God, saying, 'Shall I go up against the Philistines? And wilt thou give them into my hand?' Then the Lord said to him, 'Go up, for I will give them into your hand.' And the Philistines made yet another raid in the valley. And David inquired again of God, and God said to him, 'You shall not go up after them; circle around behind them, and come at them in front of the balsam trees."

David had to ask each time and God did not allow him to develop a system; he had to stay in contact with the Lord.

When Jesus healed the blind He touched their eyes (Mt 9:29); spoke to them (Mark 10:52); and mixed spittle with clay (Jn 9:6). This keeps us from becoming ritualistic; He talks to us personally and uses different methods at different times.

Day 137 I Chr 17-19; Mt 13-14; Ps 79-81

Ps 80:8-9 "Thou didst remove a vine from Egypt; thou didst drive out the nations, and didst plant it. Thou didst clear the ground before it, and it took deep root and filled the land."

Mt 21:33 "Listen to another parable. There was a landowner who planted a vineyard and put a wall around it, dug a winepress in it and built a tower, and rented it out to vine-growers and went on a journey."

He sent servants, then he sent other servants and then he sent his son whom they killed. This is not about Israel only, we are all responsible for the death of Jesus. He died for the sins of all mankind past, present and future. We have been planted and He expects an increase. I read an article that said the Jews killed Jesus, how ignorant!

Heb 12:2 "…for the joy that was set before Him endured the cross…;" without His death we could not have been redeemed. Now we are the people God has grafted in, He has set a hedge around us, now it is time to produce for Him.

Acts 6:7 "And the word of God kept on spreading, and the number of the disciples continued to increase greatly in Jerusalem, and a great many of the priests were becoming obedient to the faith."

The first command of the Lord to Adam was to be fruitful and multiply.

Day 138 I Chr 20-23; Mt 15-16; Ps 82-84

I Chr 21:1 "Then Satan stood up against Israel, and moved David to number Israel."

I didn't find in the laws established from God anything about taking a census being a sin. But God is our strength and Israel was not to depend on their numbers for strength.

Judges 7:2 "And the Lord said to Gideon, 'The people who are with you are too many for Me to give Midian into their hands, lest Israel become boastful, saying, 'My own power has delivered me.'"

This is like people thinking they can be good enough to be saved in their own power. There is nothing we can do but trust in Jesus.

David sinned and all Israel was punished. The seer, Gad came to David and told him God was giving him a choice of punishment, three years of famine, three months being defeated by his enemies or three days of plague. David chose to fall into the hands of God "for His mercies are very great" I Chr 21:13 and the plague killed seventy thousand men.

Day 139 I Chr 24-26; Mt 17-18; Ps 85-87

Mt 10:1 "And having summoned His twelve disciples, He gave them authority over unclean spirits, to cast them out, and to heal every kind of disease and every kind of sickness."

I remember being told in school that ignorant people blamed things they couldn't understand onto evil spirits. This is actually a strong spirit of unbelief which is over our country and very subtle. Many have prayed for years for a family member to be saved when they should have been also binding the 'spirit of unbelief' which has darkened the mind.

Mt 17:14 16 & 20 21 "And when they came to the multitude, a man came up to Him, falling on his knees before Him, and saying, 'Lord have mercy on my son, for he is a lunatic, and is very ill; for he often falls into the water." And I brought him to Your disciples, and they could not cure him." After rebuking the demon, it came out and the child was cured. When asked why they could not cast the demon out, Jesus answered, "Because of the littleness of your faith…..But this kind does not go out except by prayer and fasting."

Day 140 I Chr 27-29; Mt 19-20; Ps 88-90

Mt 19:3-12 The Pharisees came to test Jesus by asking about divorce. Jesus told them that from the beginning man and woman became one. "Consequently they are no longer two but one flesh.

What therefore God has joined together let no man separate."

The Essential Word

Anyone who divorces except for sexual immorality commits adultery and anyone who marries her who is divorced commits adultery. "The disciples said to Him, 'If the relationship of the man with his wife, is like this, it is better not to marry.' But He said to them, 'Not all men can accept this statement, but only those to whom it has been given; for there are eunuchs who were born that way from their mother's womb, and there are eunuchs who were made eunuchs by men, and there are eunuchs who have made themselves eunuchs for the sake of the kingdom of heaven. He who is able to accept it, let him accept it."

I Cor 7:5 & 7-9 Paul commenting on marriage said to not deprive one another except for a time of fasting and prayer. "Yet I wish that all men were even as I myself am. However, each man has his own gift from God, one in this manner and another in that. But I say to the unmarried and to the widows, that it is good for them if they remain even as I. But if they do not have self-control, let them marry; for it is better to marry than to burn."

Paul being unmarried could devote every minute to serving the Lord and travel where the Spirit led. Don't try to follow the ministry of others, let God show you His plan.

Day 141 II Chr 1-3; Mt 21-22; Ps 91-93

Mt 21:4-5 "Now this took place that what was spoken through the prophet, might be fulfilled, saying, Zech 9:9 'Say to the daughter of Zion, Behold your King is coming to you, gentle, and mounted on a donkey, even on a colt, the foal of a beast of burden."

Is 62:11-12 "Behold the Lord has proclaimed to the end of the earth, say to the daughter of Zion, 'Lo your salvation comes; behold, His reward is with Him, and His recompense before Him' and they will call them the holy people, the redeemed of the Lord; and you will be called 'Sought out, a city not forsaken."

Gen 49:10-11 "The scepter shall not depart from Judah, nor a ruler's staff from between his feet, until Shiloh comes; and to Him shall be the obedience of the peoples. He ties his donkey to the vine, and his donkey's colt to the choice vine, He washes his garments in wine, and his robes in the blood of grapes.

This was written because the blood of the grape represents the Blood of Jesus. The word Shiloh refers to the Messiah and means: tranquil, i.e. secure or successful: --be happy, prosper, be in safety.

Day 142 II Chr 4-7; Mt 23-24; Ps 94-96

I have heard so many say that they wished they could have walked with Jesus and sat at His feet to hear Him teach. If I had walked the streets of Jerusalem in the time of Jesus, would I have been a believer or would I have been one of the multitude who shouted, "Crucify Him, crucify Him?" I am glad that I have a closer walk than was available to His disciples when they walked with Him. They did not truly know Him until after He was resurrected. Then they understood His purpose in coming to earth and received power through the Holy Spirit.

John 16:7 & 14:26 "But I tell you the truth. It is to your advantage that I go away; for if I go not away, the helper shall not come to you; but if I go, I will send Him unto you.…..But the Helper, the Holy Spirit, whom the Father will send in My name, He will teach you all things, and bring to your remembrance all that I said to you." (KJV)

Mark 13:11 "And when they arrest you and deliver you up, do not be anxious beforehand about what you are to say, but say whatever is given you in that hour, for it is not you who speak, but it is the Holy Spirit."

Day 143 II Chr 8-10; Mt 25-26; Ps 97-99

II Chr 8:7-8 "All the people who were left of the Hittites, Amorites, Perizzites, Hivites, and Jebusites, who were not of Israel, namely, from their descendants who were left after them in the land, whom the sons of Israel had not destroyed, them Solomon raised as forced laborers to this day."

De 20:16-18 "Only in the cities of these peoples that the Lord your God is giving you as an inheritance, you shall not leave alive anything that breathes. But you shall utterly destroy them, the Hittite and the Amorite, the Canaanite and the Perizzite, the Hivite and the Jebusite, as the Lord your God has commanded you, in order that they may not teach you to do according to all their detestable things which they have done for their gods, so that you would sin against the Lord your God."

These people were not destroyed totally and continued to bring the Israelites back to idol worship and sin time after time.

Day 144 II Chr 11-13; Mt 27-28; Ps 100-102

II Chr 11 After the death of Solomon the kingdom was divided; Rehoboam was king of Judah (which included Benjamin). Jeroboam (from the tribe of Ephraim) was king of the other ten tribes.

Jeroboam and his sons rejected the Lord's priests, so the Levites left their common-lands and their possessions and came to Judah.

I Chr 11:15 "And he (Jeroboam) set up priests of his own for the high places, for the satyrs, and for the calves which he had made."

Romans 1:22-23 "Professing to be wise, they became fools, and exchanged the glory of the incorruptible God for an image in the form of corruptible man---and of birds and four-footed animals and crawling creatures."

II Chr 12:1-2 & 7-8 Rehoboam after building up his kingdom turned, so that "he and all Israel with him forsook the law of the Lord." The Lord brought Egypt against them and they repented. "And when the Lord saw that they humbled themselves, the word of the Lord came to Shemaiah, saying, 'They have humbled themselves; so I will not destroy them, but I will grant them some measure of deliverance …. But they will become his slaves so that they may learn the difference between My service and the service of the kingdoms of the countries."

Day 145 II Chr 14-16; Mark 1-2; Ps 103-105

II Chr 14:2-6 & 11-13 King Asa did what was right and sought the Lord, the Lord gave Judah rest. He built fortifications for the cities during the time of peace and had an army of five hundred and eighty thousand. Then Zerah the Ethiopian came out against them with a much larger army.

"Then Asa called to the lord his God, and said, 'Lord, there is no one besides Thee to help in the battle between the powerful and those who have no strength; so help us, O Lord our God, for we trust in Thee, and in Thy name have come against this multitude. O Lord, Thou art our God; let not man prevail against Thee. So the Lord routed the Ethiopians before Asa and before Judah, and the Ethiopians fled."

II Chr 16:7-9 In the thirty-sixth year of Asa's reign the king of Israel attacked and Asa sent a bribe to the king of Syria for help. "At that time Hanani the seer came to Asa king of Judah and said to him, "Because you have relied on the king of Aram and have not relied on the Lord your God, therefore the army of the king of Aram has escaped out of your hand. Were the Ethiopians and the Lubim not an immense army with very many chariots and horsemen? Yet, because you relied on the Lord, He delivered them into your hand. For the eyes of the Lord run to and fro throughout the earth, that He may strongly support those whose heart is completely His. You have acted foolishly in this. Indeed, from now on you will surely have wars."

What does this tell us about the battles in our life? Poor Asa, he started out so strong and then fizzled.

When he became diseased in his feet, he did not seek the Lord, but the physicians.

Day 146 II Chr 17-19; Mark 3-4; Ps 106-108

II Chr 17 Jehoshaphat became king and followed the way of his father in Asa's early days. He sent Levites and other spiritual leaders out to teach the commandments of the Lord to the people. And the fear of the Lord fell on the nations around them so that no wars were declared against Judah.

II Chr 18:2 The traps of Satan are very subtle, when Jehoshaphat met Ahab, king of Israel; and Ahab asks him to go into battle with Israel, it just seemed the right thing to do. Judah hadn't had a fight for so long and had all those men ready for war. Israel and Judah were all the sons of Jacob, you know, family. Israel, however, was not their brother in the Spirit. Ahab worshipped idols and did not follow the Lord. Ahab died in the battle.

II Chr 19:1-4 The prophet, Jehu told Jehoshaphat that he should not help the ungodly, and love them who hate the Lord, but because there was good in him, he ruled in peace after returning to Judah.

Day 147 II Chr 20-22; Mark 5-6; Ps 109-111

Moab and Ammon, sons of Lot, and Mt Seir, the descendants of Esau, came to attack Judah. Judah was vastly outnumbered and cried out to the Lord.

II Chr 20:15 & 17 They were told: "Listen, all Judah and the inhabitants of Jerusalem, and King Jehoshaphat! Thus says the Lord to you, 'Do not fear or be dismayed because of this great multitude, for the battle is not yours, but God's. You need not fight in this battle; station yourselves, stand still and see the salvation of the Lord, on your behalf, O Judah and Jerusalem! Do not fear or be dismayed; tomorrow go out to face them, for the Lord is with you."

Then they worshiped. The next day they went to meet the enemy, singing praises. When they went, they found dead bodies and it took three days to gather up all the spoil. They came back to Jerusalem worshiping and the fear of them fell on the other nations and they had peace for a time.

We don't really want all people to fear us, but the demons we come against when wrestling for the soul of that person the Lord has given us a burden for, yes they should be afraid because we are coming for their captive.

Day 148 II Chr 23-25; Mark 7-8; Ps 112-114

II Chr 23:6 Only the priest could enter the house of the Lord. In Mt 27:51; the veil is torn so that all may enter, not just the temple, but the Holy of Holies. All believers in Jesus may enter into the presence of God, without barriers except by our own reluctance. We separate ourselves because of sin and being caught up in worldly activities that consumes great chunks of time.

Eph 5:14-16 "For this reason it says, 'Awake, sleeper, and arise from the dead, and Christ will shine on you.' Therefore be careful how you walk, not as unwise men, but as wise, making the most of your time, because the days are evil."

The world is filled with distractions. Entertainment abounds. If God requires a tithe, is that only money or does He also require a tenth of our time? I don't know that He asks for a tenth of our time, but I do know that we will be rewarded for every minute we spend with Him. Actually, we are to abide with Him. Abide: 3427- dwell, to remain; cause to settle, to marry.

Day 149 II Chr 26-28; Mark 9-10; Ps 115-117

II Chr 26:3-5 & 16 "Uzziah was 16 years old when he became king, … he did right in the sight of the Lord, according to all that his father Amaziah had done. He continued to seek God in the days of Zechariah, who had understanding through the visions of God; and as long as he sought the Lord, God made him prosper." "But when he was strong his heart was lifted up to his destruction for he transgressed…"

Ps 147:6 "The Lord lifteth up the meek (humble); He casteth the wicked down to the ground." (KJV)

Ez 28:17 When Lucifer was cast out of heaven, the Lord said: "Your heart was lifted up because of your beauty; you corrupted your wisdom by reason of your splendor; I cast you to the ground; I put you before kings, that they may gaze at you."

How sad, for Uzziah, a man who followed God for so long to let arrogance take hold of him. But, it happened to so many of the kings. He went into the temple to burn incense to the Lord and became furious when the priests confronted him. He was struck with leprosy and spent the rest of his life in an isolated house.

The Essential Word ▮▮▮▮ 125

Day 150 II Chr 29-31; Mark 11-12; Ps 118-120

Prayer is talking to the best friend you can ever have in this world or the world to come. We often try to make it like speaking to a stranger, maybe from a foreign land. You know, like you speak slowly in simple words so they will understand.

Mark 11:17 "And He began to teach and say to them, 'Is it not written, My house shall be called a house of prayer for all the nations? But you have made it a robbers' den."

Mark 11:24-26 "Therefore I say to you, all things for which you pray and ask, believe that you have received them, and they shall be granted you. And whenever you stand praying, forgive, if you have anything against anyone, so that your Father also who is in heaven may forgive you your trespasses. But if you do not forgive, neither will your Father who is in heaven forgive your trespasses."

I John 2:3 To have prayers answered we have to: know Him, obey His commandments and hold no unforgiveness in our heart. He is able to answer every request, but are we able to meet the requirements? It is possible, but not so easy.

Day 151 II Chr 32-34; Mark 13-14; Ps 121-123

Ps 121:2 & 3 "My help comes from the Lord, who made heaven and earth. He will not allow your foot to slip;"

Jn 10:27-28 "My sheep hear My voice, and I know them, and they follow Me; and I give eternal life to them, and they shall never perish; and no one shall snatch them out of My hand."

No one can remove us from the hand of God, but we can jump. By disobedience and bitterness and unforgiveness we pack our baggage and move out and we are left with our baggage. The Amplified Bible gives a more complete meaning to the word, believe—"-adhere to, trust in and rely on the truth."

There are many people who believe there is a God, but do not know the Son, but the God they acknowledge is mysterious and far from them.

Pr 18:24 "A man of many friends comes to ruin, but there is a friend who sticks closer than a brother."

That friend is Jesus.

Day 152 II Chr 35-Ezra 1; Mark 15-16; Ps 124-126

Ezra 1:2 "Thus says Cyrus king of Persia; 'The Lord the God of heaven, has given me all the kingdoms of the earth, and He has appointed me to build Him a house in Jerusalem which is in Judah."

Is 44:24 & 28 "Thus says the Lord, your Redeemer,...Who says of Cyrus, 'He is My shepherd! And he will perform all My desire. And he declares of Jerusalem, 'Your foundation will be built, and of the temple, 'Your foundation will be laid."

Cyrus was a Persian king, but he knew that the God of Israel was with Israel, even in captivity. The Lord spoke to Cyrus and Cyrus obeyed. To obey without hesitation is very hard for us who have our own agenda. But it is better to follow the Lord into the unknown than to follow the well-lighted path of our own devising.

Day 153 Ezra 2-4; Luke 1-2; Ps 127-129

Luke 1:11-66 We have to think of Abraham and Sarah; how in their old age they were promised and received a son according to the Word of the Lord. Zacharias and Elizabeth didn't even have the promise to hold on to, but they were faithful to the Lord. When the angel Gabriel told Zacharias that he and Elizabeth would have a son, he didn't laugh like Sarah but asked for assurance. Because he doubted, Zacharias was unable to speak until after the birth of John. It was a sign to him and all the people who saw that he had seen a vision. On the eighth day when the baby was to be circumcised and given a name, the people said he would be named Zacharias after his father. Elizabeth said his name would be John. Before they would listen to her, they asked Zacharias and he wrote. "His name is John" and his mouth was opened and he gave praise to God. The name John is derived from the Hebrew "Jonathan" and means Jehovah-favored. Fear came on the people who lived around them and they wondered what kind of child this would be.

Day 154 Ezra 5-7; Luke 3-4; Ps 130-132

Ps 129 Israel was attacked again and again. The enemies on every side would gather and attack. Women and children would be snatched and taken away to be slaves, men killed in battle. Peace was always temporary. David, because he had a heart of worship, had less defeat than many other kings. He still had a sin nature which brought trouble to him, so he could say, "They have afflicted me.... but they did not prevail."

We cannot be defeated from the outside, only by our own weakness. Jesus was tempted when He was weakened after forty days of fasting. When He was hungry, Satan was there. When David was alone and weak, there was Bathsheba.

The genealogy in Luke 3:23-38, is of Joseph, and in Mt 1:1-16 is of Mary. It is unusual for the women to be mentioned in genealogies, but both were descendants of David.

Day 155 Ezra 8-10; Luke 5-6; Ps 133-135

II K 24:1-4 & 13 Nebuchadnezzar, King of Babylon came against Jehoiakim and the Lord caused this to remove Judah from Jerusalem, because of sin and the innocent blood they had shed. And Nebuchadnezzar took all Judah and all the treasures of the house of the Lord. After their captivity in Babylon, they were being allowed to return.

Ezra 9:1 Leaders came and told Ezra, "The people of Israel and the priests and the Levites have not separated themselves from the peoples of the lands, according to their abominations, those of the Canaanites, the Hittites, the Perizzites, the Jebusites, the Ammonites, the Moabites, the Egyptians and the Amorites." Four of these tribes were listed in Gen 15:18-21. People they were supposed to drive out completely and not pollute themselves with them or their idol worship. They had taken wives from these heathen peoples. After fasting and praying, it was agreed that the pagan wives and children should be sent away, so the people of Judah could come back into right relation to the Lord.

To come back to the Lord sinful relationships have to be broken.

Day 156 Neh 1-3; Luke 7-8; Ps 136-138

Ezra 7:7 Ezra returned to Jerusalem in the seventh year of king Artaxerxes.

Neh 2 Nehemiah was cup bearer in the twentieth year of King Artaxerxes when he was given the news that Jerusalem was in bad shape with the walls broken down and the gates burned. The king saw his sorrow and gave Nehemiah permission to go and sent letters with him so he could pass safely until he came to Judah and get materials to repair the wall and gates. Ezra and Nehemiah were both given grace from pagan kings because the Lord's time had come. The priests and men of Jerusalem worked; each section was completed by a small group until the sections were joined.

Eph 4:16 "from whom the whole body, being fitted and held together by that which every joint supplies, according to the proper working of each individual part, causes the growth of the body for the building up of itself in love."

Israel was punished for sin many times and it was harsh but when they humbled themselves and asked for forgiveness God was ready to give them mercy.

Day 157 Neh 4-6; Luke 9-10; Ps 139-141

Neh 4:11 & 14 & 16-17 Enemies rose up who did not want Judah to be established again, and they came to kill the workers that were building the walls. Nehemiah said, "Do not be afraid of them. Remember the Lord, great and awesome, and fight for your brethren," "And it came about from that day on, that half of my servants carried on the work while half of them held the spears, the shields, the bows and the breastplates; and the captains were behind the whole house of Judah. Those who were rebuilding the wall and those who carried burdens took their load with one hand doing the work and the other holding a weapon."

Eph 4:4, 11-13 "There is one body and one Spirit, just as also you were called in one hope of your calling; And He Himself gave some apostles, and some as prophets, and some as evangelists, and some as pastors and teachers, for the equipping of the saints for the work of service, to the building up of the body of Christ, until we all attain to the unity of the faith and of the knowledge of the Son of God"

Whether you carry a spear or carry stones, every calling has its own value to the Lord.

Day 158 Neh 7-9; Luke 11-12; Ps 142-144

Luke 11:17-18 "… any kingdom divided against itself is laid waste; and a house divided against itself falls. And if Satan also is divided against himself, how shall his kingdom stand?"

It is true for Satan's domain and it is also true of the Lords kingdom. The early church was like a tornado, they turned the world upside down. If they were thrown into prison, they brought the light of Jesus to that dark place.

I Cor 12:27 "Now you are Christ's body and individually members of it."

I Cor 1:10 "Now I exhort you brethren, by the name of our Lord Jesus Christ, that you all agree, and there be no divisions among you, but you be made complete in the same mind and in the same judgment."

There are many denominations with doctrinal differences. If we all had a sound understanding of the Holy Bible instead of the doctrines of men, petty arguments would disappear like misty fog when the light of the 'Son of Righteousness' shines.

Day 159 Neh 10-12; Luke 13-14; Ps 145-147

Luke 13:6-9 Jesus told a parable about a man who planted a fig tree and it did not produce fruit for three years. He told the keeper to cut it down, but the keeper asked for another year of grace and the ground would be worked up and fertilizer applied. Then if the tree did not produce figs they would cut it down. The keeper in the Lords vineyard is the Holy Spirit who takes our hand to lead us, if we are stubborn He pulls us and if we will not go then He uses the rod of correction. We suffer so much because of willfulness. If we remain stubborn, then we are removed from the Lords vineyard.

Ps 1 "How blessed is the man.... whose delight is in the Law of the Lord. He will be like a tree firmly planted by the streams of water, which yields its fruit in its season, and its leaf does not wither; and in whatever he does, he prospers. The wicked are not so but they are like chaff which the wind drives away".

Day 160 Neh 13-Esther 2; Luke 15-16; Ps 148-150

Neh 2:6 Nehemiah was a Jewish prisoner in Babylon who served the King as cup bearer (it was the custom for a cupbearer to have the duty of drinking the first of the cup to make sure that the king was not poisoned). They had a relationship of trust and caring, for the king when he saw that Nehemiah was sad, gave Nehemiah permission to return to Jerusalem for a time to rebuild the walls, and then he returned.

Neh 13:6 & 4 "But during all this time I was not in Jerusalem, for in the thirty-second year of Artaxerxes king of Babylon I had gone to the king. After some time, however, I asked leave from the king,"

While Nehemiah was absent from Jerusalem, having authority over the storerooms of the temple, Eliashib the priest, took a large room for Tobiah (an Ammorite); and the grain, frankincense and the articles of worship, etc. were removed.

Neh 13:7-8 "and I came to Jerusalem and learned about the evil that Eliashib had done for Tobiah, by preparing a room for him in the courts of the house of God. And it was very displeasing to me, so I threw all of Tobiah's household goods out of the room."

This is very like Jesus clearing the temple.

Day 161 Esther 3-5; Luke 17-18; Ps 1-3

John 15:18 "If the world hates you, you know that it has hated Me before it hated you." The Jews are so hated by those who hate the Lord. How many times has there been an attempt to totally kill every Jew? Not so long ago there were Hitler and Stalin. Now there is the Muslim threat, in their hatred, they blame the Jews for every problem. Although there is so much suffering, they always fail.

God's purpose for Israel will not be changed. Mordecai did not bow to a petty little man who thought he was someone great, so Haman plotted to kill every Jew because of this slight. When Mordecai told Esther to speak to the king, she was fearful.

Esther 4:13-14 "Then Mordecai told them to reply to Esther: 'Do not imagine that you in the king's palace can escape any more than all the Jews. For if you remain silent at this time, relief and deliverance will arise for the Jews from another place and you and your father's house will perish. And who knows whether you have not attained royalty for such a time as this?"

The Lord had plans for you and me before we were born, will we recognize our purpose before it's too late?

Day 162 Esther 6-8; Luke 19-20; Ps 4-6

Pr 21:1 "The king's heart is like channels of water in the hand of the Lord; He turns it wherever He wishes."

God used Esther because, although she was fearful, she was available. There are many ways to fast, the Esther fast was three days and nights with no food or water. The night before the second banquet that Esther was giving for the king and Haman, the king couldn't sleep. He didn't call for one of his wives, nor soft music. He commanded for the book of records to be read to him. He was reminded that Mordecai had saved his life and not been rewarded

Pr 18:12 "Before destruction the heart of a man is haughty, but humility goes before honor."

Haman came into the court to request that Mordecai should be hanged, but honor was given to Mordecai instead and Haman was humiliated. Jesus warned that we should not exalt ourselves, but wait for others to give us honor.

Luke 14:8-10 "When you are invited by someone to a wedding feast, do not take the place of honor, lest someone more distinguished than you may have been invited by him, and he who invited you both shall come and say to you, 'Give place to this man, and then in disgrace you proceed to occupy the last place. But when you are invited, go and recline at the last place, so that when the one who has invited you comes, he may say to you, 'Friend, move up higher'; then you will have honor in the sight of all who are at the table with you."

I Pet 5:5-6 "...God is opposed to the proud, but gives grace to the humble. Therefore humble yourselves under the mighty hand of God, that He may exalt you in due time."

Again, a plot to kill all Jews came back on the heads of those who hate the Lord.

Day 163 Esther 9-Job 1; Luke 21-22; Ps 7-9

Job 1 Job was a man who was blameless and upright. How are we attacked by Satan? Sin in our life opens the door for attack. We get angry, hold a grudge, envy others who seem to be more blessed, have unclean thoughts, etc. But here is Job. People around him thought he was righteous, but they couldn't see the heart. The lord sees the heart, and He said Job was blameless and upright! He was very wealthy, but in one day his oxen, donkeys, sheep, camels, and all ten of his children were gone. All his servants from the fields were dead except four because in every attack one person was left to take Job the bad news so that it hit him all at one time. He tore his robe, shaved his head and fell down and worshiped. That is complete trust, in all his grief he did not sin. Since Job was sinless, Satan had to get permission like he did for Simon Peter.

Luke 22:31-32 "Simon. Simon, behold Satan has demanded permission to sift you like wheat; but I have prayed for you,..."

Why does the Lord give permission? Paul gives us one possibility

II Cor12:7 "And because of the surpassing greatness of the revelations, for this reason to keep me from exalting myself, there was given me a thorn in the flesh, a messenger of Satan to buffet me---to keep me from exalting myself!"

Day 164 Job 2-4; Luke 23-24; Ps 10-12

There is no sign that Job understood why calamity had fallen on him, but he accepted it.

Job 1:21 "Naked I came from my mother's womb, and naked I shall return there. The Lord gave and the Lord has taken away; blessed be the name of the Lord."

Job 2:10 "Shall we indeed accept good from God, and not accept adversity?"

Job's friend Eliphaz, was a wise man and spoke of things that were mostly accurate by the laws of nature, but he presumed to know the mind of God.

Job 4:7-8 & 17-19 Eliphaz said, "Remember now, who ever perished being innocent? Or where were the upright destroyed? According to what I have seen, those who plow iniquity and those sow trouble harvest it." "Can mankind be just before God? Can a man be pure before his Maker? He puts no trust even in His servants; and against His angels He charges error. How much more those who dwell in houses of clay, whose foundation is in the dust, ..." referring to the fall of Satan and the creation of Adam. The Lord had to set them all straight.

Job is considered to be the oldest written book in the Bible because Moses wrote Genesis through Deuteronomy under the inspiration of God.

Day 165 Job 5-7; John 1-2; Ps 13-15

John 1:1 & 5 & 11 In the beginning was Jesus, who became God's message of love to us. "And the light shines in the darkness and the darkness did not comprehend it. He came to His own, and those who were His own did not receive Him."

It is so amazing that more of the people did not recognize Jesus when He started His ministry. They were God's chosen people with a history that was so miraculous, so astounding and prophecies to lead them in the dark. The religious leaders were blinded by selfishness in trying to protect their wealth and position of high honor, which is the reason most of His followers were the poor and sick and disabled. But even after we have come to Jesus and begun to learn His way, we still have so much darkness to fumble our way through.

I Cor 13:9 & 12 "For we know in part and we prophesy in part. For now we see in a mirror, dimly, but then face to face; now I know in part, but then I shall know fully just as I also have been fully known."

Day 166 Job 8-10; John 3-4; Ps 16-18

John 3:19-20 "And this is the judgment, that the light has come into the world, and men loved the darkness rather than the light; for their deeds were evil. For everyone evil hates the light and does not come to the light, lest his deeds should be exposed."

Job 24:13, 15 &16 "Others have been with those who rebel against the light, they do not want to know its ways, nor abide in its paths. And the eye of the adulterer waits for the twilight, saying, 'No eye will see me.' And he disguises his face. In the dark they dig into houses, they shut themselves up by day; they do not know the light."

But, their time will end; they will not do evil forever.

Is 2:12 & 19 "For the Lord of hosts will have a day of reckoning against everyone who is proud and lofty, and against everyone who is lifted up, that he may be abased. And men will go into the caves of the rocks and into holes of the ground before the terror of the Lord, and before the splendor of His majesty."

We must seek the light.

Is 55:6-7 "Seek the Lord while He may be found, call upon Him while He is near. Let the wicked forsake his way, and the unrighteous man his thoughts; and let him return to the Lord, and He will have compassion on him; and to our God for He will abundantly pardon.

Day 167 Job 11-13; John 5-6; Ps 19-21

Job 11 The friends of Job are trying to correct his thinking. Zophar thinks that Job should admit to a secret sin that has brought so much punishment from the Lord.

It is true that we bring bad things down on our heads through sin, there is still the law of sowing and reaping. But, doing everything that you can to live an upright life, you will still have problems because we are in a sinful world that is cursed. We are living in a fallen world. Nature takes its toll and if we don't die young we will all get old and probably very sick. So, how are we better off than the unbelievers?

Because we have peace and trust in the Lord, every trial is lighter, so much lighter, except one, our burden for the lost. We carry the pain of the ones we love rebelling against God. But even in that burden we have a Father that listens. And if we are persistent, He will answer.

Ps 9:9 -10 "The Lord also will be a stronghold for the oppressed, a stronghold in times of trouble. And those who know Thy name will put their trust in Thee; for Thou hast not forsaken those who seek Thee." We are never alone.

Day 168 Job 14-16; John 7-8; Ps 22-24

Ps 22:1 & 6-18 This is Jesus on the cross. When the sin of all mankind was put on Jesus, the Father turned His face away. He was despised and ridiculed and mocked by the people He loved. His hands and feet were nailed down, and the bulls of Bashan are demons that tortured Him as He hung helpless.

As he dehydrated His bones were disjointed and vital organs shut down. The paintings of Jesus shows Him covered, but the tradition was to humiliate them as much as possible and hang them naked for everyone to gape at. What amazing love that He has for us.

Heb 12:2-4 "Fixing our eyes on Jesus, the author and perfecter of our faith, who for the joy set before Him endured the cross, despising the shame, and has sat down at the right hand of the throne of God. For consider Him who endured such hostility by sinners against Himself, so that you may not grow weary and lose heart. You have not yet resisted to the point of shedding blood in your striving against sin."

Day 169 Job 17-19; John 9-10; Ps 25-27

The Pharisees were very religious, following the Law of Moses and stacks of rules that had been added over many years. They had hedged themselves in with the physical of 'do this and don't do that' which never touch the heart. Jesus brings us into a relationship with Himself and asks for us to love the Lord and our neighbor as we love ourselves. (The Jewish translation is "Love your neighbor as God loves him)

The rules of the Pharisees were cold and comfortless.

II Kings 22:11 When King Josiah heard the words of the Book of Moses which had been lost for a long time, he realized how far they had veered from the true course.

John 9:4-7 But, by the time of Jesus, empty religion had prevailed again, and they were outraged that Jesus would heal a man blind from birth on the Sabbath. The man had no value to them, they only cared about their traditions.

Day 170 Job 20-22; John 11-12; Ps 28-30

I Cor 15:21-22 "For since by man came death, by a man also came the resurrection of the dead. For as in Adam all die, so in Christ all shall be made alive."

Mary and Martha had heard the wonderful teachings and seen Jesus do amazing miracles. When their brother Lazarus became sick, they sent for Jesus, but Jesus didn't come. Lazarus died and was buried. Finally Jesus came to Bethany. He let Lazarus die and be buried for four days to reveal His resurrection power and told Martha that He actually was the RESURRECTION! After Lazarus walked out of the tomb, people flocked to see Lazarus, to hear eyewitness accounts.

John 12:10-11 "But the chief priests took council to put Lazarus to death also, because on account of him many of the Jews were going away and were believing in Jesus."

The people are drawn to love and compassion and they saw that in Jesus, if we can show these attributes people will be drawn to the Spirit of God in us.

Day 171 Job 23-25; John 13-14; Ps 31-33

There are the Ten Commandments in Ex 20:3-17. The unbeliever would think God just doesn't want them to have any fun, but these are for our protection. Idol worship was degrading and the cause of many diseases and strife. Obedience brought harmony in relationships and peace.

But a lawyer testing Jesus asked a question.

Mt 22:36-40 "Teacher, which is the great commandment in the law?' And He said to him, 'You shall love the Lord your God with all your heart, with all your soul, and with all your mind, this is the first and foremost commandment. And the second is like it; 'You shall love your neighbor as yourself. On these two commandments depend the whole Law and the Prophets."

Jn 13:34-35 "A new commandment I give to you, that you love one another; as I have loved you, that you also love one another. By this all men will know that you are My disciples, if you have love for one another."

Mt 5:43-44 "You have heard that it was said, 'You shall love your neighbor and hate your enemy.' But I say to you, love your enemies, and pray for those who persecute you."

This goes way beyond the original Ten Commandments.

Love is aggressive. It is a spiritual attack that goes to their heart and draws them to the Lord.

Day 172 Job 26-28; John 15-16; Ps 34-36

Jn 15:5-6 Jesus said, "I am the vine, you are the branches. He who abides in Me, and I in him bears much fruit; for apart from Me you can do nothing. If anyone does not abide in Me, he is thrown away as a branch and dries up; and they gather them and cast them into the fire, and they are burned."

Has God rejected the Jews?

Rom 11:17-18 "And if some of the branches were broken off, and you, being a wild olive tree, were grafted in among them, and with them became a partaker of the rich root of the olive tree, do not be arrogant toward the branches; but if you are arrogant, remember that it is not you who supports the root, but the root supports you."

The leaders of Israel rejected Jesus and He was crucified. Not all Israel, but only the unbelieving of Israel were rejected and gentiles were grafted in, but do not be arrogant for only the humble will be accepted and

He is able to graft them in again. In nature this is impossible, but in the spirit, anything is possible. Gal 5:22-23 The fruit he desires and demands to see in us is love, joy, peace, longsuffering, kindness, goodness, faithfulness, gentleness, and self-control.

Day 173 Job 29-31; John 17-18; Ps 37-39

Job 30:1-8 Here is a description of people who live in caves and gather mallow and eat roots. They were driven away from civilized areas because they were sons of fools, sons of vile men.

The first created people had great intelligence.

Gen 4:17 "And Cain knew his wife, and she conceived and bore Enoch. And he built a city, and called the name of the city after the name of his son--Enoch." Knowledge is built and added to, as we learn by doing. The sons of Lamech were Jabel who was a herdsman, Jubal who played the harp and flute, Tubal-Cain was an instructor of every craftsman in bronze and iron. Who taught Cain how to build a city?

Who taught these men seven generations from Adam how to create these things? Adam was created in the image of God, body and mind. The early people were very intelligent, but through sin the mind and heart is darkened.

Rom 1:21-22 "For even though they knew God, they did not honor Him as God, or give thanks, but they became futile in their speculations, and their foolish hearts were darkened. Professing to be wise, they became fools."

Eph 4:17-18 "This I say, therefore, and affirm together with the Lord, that you walk no longer just as the Gentiles also walk, in the futility of their mind, being darkened in their understanding excluded from the life of God, because of the ignorance that is in them, because of the hardness of their heart,"

Jesus is the Light of the world. He broke the power of darkness.

Dan 12:4 "But you Daniel conceal these words, and seal up the book until the end of time; many shall go back and forth, and knowledge will increase,"

Knowledge has increased and speeds up the closer we are to the end. People began with super intelligence and decreased until Jesus broke the power of darkness, so intelligence increased again. But neither intelligence nor ignorance make you righteous, righteousness has to be chosen.

Day 174 Job 32-34; John 19-20; Ps 40-42

John 20:21-23 "Jesus therefore said to them again, 'Peace be with you; as the Father has sent Me, I also send you.' And when He had said this, He breathed on them, and said to them, 'Receive the Holy Spirit, if you forgive the sins of any, their sins have been forgiven them, if you retain the sins of any, they have been retained."

If I don't forgive then I am binding their sin to them. That one and I are both guilty.

Mt 18:6-7 "But whoever causes one of these little ones who believe in Me to sin, it would be better for him if a millstone were hung around his neck, and he were drowned in the depth of the sea. Woe to the world because of offenses! For offenses must come, but woe to that man by whom the offense comes!"

If we do not forgive, we are not forgiven and the person who caused us to stumble will not be forgiven for the cause of our fall. I don't believe that we have the power to send someone to eternal hell, but we will all stand before the judgment seat of Christ to be judged for our deeds.

Day 175 Job 35-37; John 21-Acts 1; Ps 43-45

Ps 44:5-8 "Through Thee we will push back our adversaries; through Thy name we will trample down those who rise up against us. For I will not trust in my bow, not will my sword save me. But Thou hast saved us from our adversaries, and Thou hast put to shame those who hate us. In God we have boasted all day long, and we will give thanks to Thy name forever.

After great victory, we will very likely become complaisant and the Lord in faithfulness has to bring correction. We forget that He is our strength and begin to think we are something great. The pattern repeats blessing followed by cursing, coming to repentance and acknowledging our dependence to come back to the place of blessing. It took forty years for God to release Israel from the wilderness after they had rejected the Lord as their leader.

Day 176 Job 38-40; Acts 2-3; Ps 46-48

Job 1:8 Job was, "a blameless and upright man, fearing God and turning away from evil."

But, God had to let Job know that he lacked knowledge.

Job 38:2-9 "Who is this who darkens counsel by words without knowledge? Where were you when I laid the foundations of the earth ….On what were its bases sunk? Or who laid its cornerstone…. when I made a cloud its garment?"

I read and study, I look into the root words to search for better understanding, but the Lord is so far above us. It is like trying to teach a six month old baby how to repair the car. Paul was more blessed than most of the early evangelists, being a Pharisee he had a sound knowledge of the scriptures (Old Testament).

II Cor 12:4 Furthermore, he spoke of a man (supposedly himself) who was "caught up into Paradise and heard inexpressible words, which a man is not permitted to speak." This is so similar to Moses who spent 40 days on a mountain with God and was shown the patterns in heaven. They were given exceptional knowledge because their mission was exceptional.

Day 177 Job 41-Is 1; Acts 4-5; Ps 49-51

Isaiah was prophet in the time of Uzziah, Jotham, Ahaz and Hezekiah kings of Judah.

The Essential Word ▐▐▐▐   147

Is 1:24-25 "Therefore the Lord God of hosts, the Mighty One of Israel declares,....I will turn my hand against you, and will smelt away your dross as with lye, and will remove your alloy."

When metal is melted, the impurities float to the top and the dross scum is removed; an alloy is created by mixing two or more metals. Where Israel always got into trouble was in adding to their religious ceremonies; go the temple and offer their sacrifices to the Lord and go to the groves and give offerings to idols.

I Kings 18:18-40 Ahab accused Elijah of causing trouble in Israel. Elijah replied, "I have not troubled Israel, but you and your father's house have, because you have forsaken the commandments of the Lord, and you have followed the Baals." The 450 prophets of Baal and the people were gathered on Mount Carmel and Elijah said to them: "How long will you hesitate between two opinions? If the Lord is God, follow Him; but if Baal, follow him."

Baal flunked the test and the 450 prophets of Baal were put to death.

Day 178 Is 2-4; Acts 6-7; Ps 52-54

Is 2:2-3 "Now it will come about that in the last days, the mountain of the house of the Lord will be established as the chief of the mountains,… and all the nations will stream to it….that He may teach us concerning His ways, that we may walk in His paths."

Jesus is the Light that came to the earth in Genesis 1:3-5. Jesus is the Prophet of Deut 18:18-19.

Acts 7:37-38 Stephen reminds them, He was promised through Moses and was on Mount Sinai when Moses received the Tablets of the Law. In Exodus 3:14 God declares His name is, "I Am" and in John 8:58 "Jesus said to them, 'Truly, truly, I say to you before Abraham was born, I Am."

That was as plain as it could be said, but of course they didn't believe Him and tried to stone Him.

John 1:1-4 "In the beginning was the Word, and the Word was with God, and the Word was God. He was in the beginning with God. All things came into being by Him, and apart from Him nothing came into being that has come into being. In him was life, and the life was the light of men."

Day 179 Is 5-7; Acts 8-9; Ps 55-57

Is 5:1-4 "Now let me sing for my well-beloved a song of my beloved concerning His vineyard. My well-beloved had a vineyard on a fertile hill. And He dug it all around removed its stones, and planted it with the choicest vine. And He built a tower in the middle of it, and hewed out a wine vat in it; then He expected it to produce good grapes, but it produced only worthless ones. And now, O inhabitants of Jerusalem and men of Judah, judge; between Me and My vineyard. What more was there to do to My vineyard that I have not done in it? …."

Mark 12:1-12 When Jesus told the parable about the Lord's vineyard the Pharisees knew this scripture very well. "And they were seeking to seize Him and yet they feared the multitude; for they understood that He spoke the parable against them. So they left Him and went away."

But they plotted how they could trap Him with His own words.

Day 180 Is 8-10; Acts 10-11; Ps 58-60

Is 10:1-2 "Woe to those who enact evil statutes, and to those who constantly record unjust decisions, and rob the poor of My people of their rights, in order that widows may be their spoil, and that they may plunder the orphans."

Pr 14:34 "Righteousness exalts a nation, but sin is a disgrace to any people."

Our nation and others are in trouble because the governments have run amuck and because the Church is not a strong influence. If this pattern continues, we will be as Israel was, when they were overrun by the Assyrians. The Lord is just and will bring judgment on us when needed. He used the Assyrian king to turn Israel from their sin, but will also punish that king because of his arrogance.

Isaiah 10: 12 & 15 "So it will be that when the Lord has completed all His work on Mount Zion and on Jerusalem, He will say, 'I will punish the fruit of the arrogant heart of the king of Assyria and the pomp of his haughtiness. Is the axe to boast itself over the one who chops with it? Is the saw to exalt itself over the one who wields it? …."

Day 181 Is 11-13; Acts 12-13; Ps 61-63

Ps 63:1-2 "O God, You art My God; I shall seek Thee earnestly; my soul thirsts for Thee, my flesh yearns for Thee, in a dry and weary land where there is no water. Thus I have beheld Thee in the sanctuary, to see Thy power and Thy glory."

In our busy, even frantic rush to get through all the responsibilities of our days, it is easy to start our day without a thought for the Lord. Some time ago I was suffering from extreme exhaustion. I realized that I had not spent any personal time with the Lord for many weeks. I determined to change that and set my alarm for an hour earlier. Amazingly my energy level was higher at the end of the day. David knew the secret of success was time with the Lord and we are so blessed with his many songs of worship.

Col 3:14-16 "And above all these things put on love, which is the perfect bond of unity. And let the peace of Christ rule in your hearts, to which indeed you were called in one body; and be thankful. Let the word of Christ richly dwell within you, with all wisdom, teaching and admonishing one another with psalms and hymns and spiritual songs, singing with thankfulness in your hearts to God."

Day 182 Is 14-16; Acts 14-15; Ps 64-66

Rev 12:4 Gabriel, Michael and Lucifer are the three archangels that are named in the Bible, if there are more we are not told but I think there are only three. When Lucifer was expelled from Heaven, a third of the angels, those under his command, went with him.

Is 14:12-14 "How you are fallen from heaven, O star of the morning, son of the dawn! You have been cut down to the earth, you who weakened the nations! But you have said in your heart: 'I will ascend to heaven; I will raise my throne above the stars of God, and I will sit on the mount of the assembly in the recesses of the north; I will ascend above the heights of the clouds, I will make myself like the Most high."

Ez 28:17 "Your heart was lifted up because of your beauty; you corrupted your wisdom by reason of your splendor; I cast you to the ground, I laid you before kings, that they may gaze at you."

He lost his beauty and his light. He lost his place of honor and he lost his place as the leader of worship in heaven.

Day 183 Is 17-19; Acts 16-17; Ps 67-69

Is 19:1 "The oracle concerning Egypt. Behold, the Lord is riding on a swift cloud, and is about to come into Egypt; the idols of Egypt will tremble at His presence, and the heart of the Egyptians will melt within them."

In the days of Moses the gods of Egypt were judged. But the same spirit is there and draws the worship now as before.

Is 19:2 "I will incite Egyptians against Egyptians; and they will each fight against his brother, city against city, kingdom against kingdom."

This could be the past, present or future. Today there is fighting everywhere in the Middle Eastern countries, group against group.

In the Bible, Egypt is a symbol for Sin. In our personal life we have to leave our worldly practices behind when we start to follow Jesus. We still have to work our job and eat to live, but our focus has had a major change, everything is seen from a different perspective.

Day 184 Is 20-22; Acts 18-19; Ps 70-72

Ps 71:4-6 "Rescue me, O my God, out of the hand of the wicked, Out of the grasp of the wrongdoer and ruthless man, for Thou art my hope, O Lord God, Thou art my confidence from my youth. By Thee I have been sustained from my birth; Thou art He who took me from my mother's womb; my praise is continually of Thee."

Though we have trouble in our lives, we can trust Him with the outcome in every situation. Love is a choice, gratitude is a choice and praise is a choice.

II Cor 10:3 "For though we walk in the flesh; we do not war according to the flesh. For the weapons of our warfare are not of the flesh but divinely powerful for the destruction of fortresses."

For what is death but going to be with the Lord?

Phil 1:21-23 "For to me, to live is Christ, and to die is gain. But if I am to live on in the flesh, this will mean fruitful labor for me; and I do not know which to choose. But I am hard-pressed from both directions, having the desire to depart and be with Christ, for that is very much better;"

Day 185 Is 23-25; Acts 20-21; Ps 73-75

Is 24:5 & 6 "The land and the earth also are defiled by their inhabitants, because they have transgressed the laws, disregarded the statutes, and broken the everlasting covenant. Therefore the curse has devoured the land and the earth, and they who dwell in it suffer the punishment…"(Amplified)

Lev 26:19-20 "And I will also break down your pride of power; I will also make your heavens like iron and your earth like bronze. And your strength shall be spent uselessly; for your land shall not yield its produce and the trees of the land shall not yield their fruit."

The Lord out of love punishes the pride of His people. If He lets us continue in error we become useless to the kingdom and even to ourselves. He uses the humble, not the arrogant. Bronze or brass represents the judgment of God. When Adam sinned and judgment was put on the land it brought forth thorns and thistles, this is a step further, that the ground produces nothing without a lot sweat.

Day 186 Is 26-28; Acts 22-23; Ps 76-78

Acts 22:1-20 Paul speaking to the Jews gave a history lesson about how he came to believe in Jesus as the Christ. But when he told them that he had been sent to the gentiles, they shouted, tore their robes and threw dust up into the air. Everywhere he went there were riots. We are too polite in our society to make such an exhibition. But the mission of the Church has not changed. The problem is that the Church is mostly ignorant of the Scriptures and lukewarm. We do not have a sense of urgency to reach the unsaved. Judgment will come on the Church and the nation if this continues.

I Peter 4:17-18 "For it is time for judgment to begin with the household of God; and if it begins with us first, what will be the outcome for those who do not obey the gospel of God? And if it is with difficulty that the righteous is saved, what will become of the godless man and sinner?"

Day 187 Is 29-31; Acts 24-25; Ps 79-81

Is 29:13-14 (Mt 15:8-9) "Then the Lord said: 'Because this people draw near with their words and honor Me with their lip service, but they remove their hearts far from Me, and their reverence for Me consists of tradition learned by rote, therefore, behold, I will once again deal marvelously with this people,"

John 13:35 "By this all men will know that you are My disciples, if you have love for one another." God is ever ready to do a new thing in all of us.

Hosea 10:12 "Sow with a view to righteousness, reap in accordance with kindness; breakup your fallow ground, for it is time to seek the Lord until He comes to rain righteousness on you." Fallow means ground that is plowed but not seeded, not in use, inactive.

I've spent way too much time being fallow and unfruitful. This can be a natural cycle, like summer and winter, but we are not called to be natural, we are called to be spiritual. You may have a time of rest but don't lay there too long, He is ready to do a marvelous work. Will you be with Him or on the sideline?

Day 188 Is 32-34; Acts 26-27; Ps 82-84

Ps 83:2-3 "For behold, Thine enemies make an uproar; and those who hate Thee have exalted themselves. They make shrewd plans against Thy people, and conspire together against Thy treasured ones."

Jesus said, that If the world hates you, you know that it hated Him before it hated you.

Those who do not worship the Lord will always be looking for a way to destroy His witness on the earth. Rev 11:3 His witnesses are Israel and the Church. Hatred has again flared up for Israel and the Church, hatred is always there but not always seen. What will be the end, it is always the same. We will suffer for a time but the end will be the confounding of God's enemies.

Ps 122:6 "Pray for the peace of Jerusalem: may they prosper who love you." At this time Jerusalem is surrounded by people who want them totally destroyed and the current administration of the United States has taken a stand against them. May God have mercy on us.

Day 189 Is 35-37; Acts 28-Rom 1; Ps 85-87

Is 35:5-6 & 9-10 "Then the eyes of the blind will be opened, and the ears of the deaf will be unstopped. Then the lame will leap like a deer, and the tongue of the dumb will shout for joy. For waters shall burst forth in the wilderness, and streams in the desert. And the ransomed of the Lord will return, and come with joyful shouting to Zion, with everlasting joy upon their heads. They will find gladness and joy; and sorrow and sighing will flee away."

Only the spiritually or willfully blind could fail to recognize Jesus. He fulfilled the prophecies so many times.

John 3:1-2 "Now there was a man of the Pharisees named Nicodemus, a ruler of the Jews; this man came to Jesus by night and said to Him, 'Rabbi, we know that you have come from God as a teacher; for no one can do these signs that You do unless God is with him."

John 19:39 Nicodemus wanted to know and understand who Jesus was; he was willing to listen, and at the end he brought myrrh and aloes for Jesus' burial.

Day 190 Is 38-40; Rom 2-3; Ps 88-90

Ps 89:1, 7, 14-16 "I will sing of the lovingkindness of the Lord forever; to all generations I will make known Thy faithfulness with my mouth. A God greatly feared in the council of the holy ones, and awesome above all those who are around Him. Righteousness and justice are the foundation of Thy throne; lovingkindness and truth go before Thee. How blessed are the people who know the joyful sound! O Lord, they walk in the light of Thy countenance. In Your name they rejoice all day long, and in Thy righteousness they are exalted."

Praise and worship draws us into the very presence of the Lord where our strength is built up again and again. If we want to be a mighty warrior for the Lord, we have to spend a lot time with Him.

Military training for battle is hard. First you have physical strength, push-ups, pull-ups and endurance, long runs and grueling marches with heavy packs. Mental readiness, knowing what to do and being ready to kill if needed.

What do we do to train for spiritual battle?

Eph 6:14-17 We must know how to use the weapons provided for us. Truth: which we learn from God's Word. Righteousness: right living according to His Word. The Gospel of peace: from His Word. Faith: which comes from hearing the Word of God. Salvation: which we learn about from His Word. The sword: which is the Word of God.

Day 191 Is 41-43; Rom 4-5; Ps 91-93

Is 41:9-10 & 14-15 "…You are My servant, I have chosen you and not rejected you. 'Do not fear, for I am with you; do not anxiously look about you, for I am your God. I will strengthen you, surely I will help you, surely I will uphold you with My righteous right hand." "Do not fear, you worm Jacob, you men of Israel; I will help you,' declares the Lord, 'and your Redeemer is the Holy One of Israel. Behold, I have made you a new, sharp threshing sledge with double edges …."

The church for the most part is a huddled mass of fear. If we mention the Lord, someone might get mad or you can get fired from your job. I know a man who didn't want to mention salvation to his sister, she might get upset. Day 64, tells about Israel coming against a fearful enemy. Their battle had a possibility of death. Our battle looks pretty puny in comparison. Of course, I don't want to suffer like the early church with stonings, beatings, etc. I think if we look for it, we can find a way to touch our world without a death sentence. But if your life is required there can be no greater cause. To leave the flesh is like stepping through a door to get into the next room where there is no pain.

Day 192 Is 44-46; Rom 6-7; Ps 94-96

Is 45 1-3 "Thus says the Lord to Cyrus His anointed, whom I have taken by the right hand, to subdue nations before him and to loose, the armor of kings, to open doors before him so that the gates will not be shut; I will go before you and make the rough places smooth; I will shatter the doors of bronze, and cut through their iron bars. I will give you the treasures of darkness and hidden wealth of secret places, that you may know that it is I, the Lord, the God of Israel, who calls you by your name."

Although Cyrus was a heathen king, God led him to fulfill his purpose to bring Jacob back to Jerusalem. Over 100 years before Cyrus was born, God knew his name and raised him up to conquer Babylon for the purpose of sending His people back to Jerusalem.

Judges 4:21 A humble woman was given an opportunity to serve Israel. The Lord sent a mighty king that was fleeing from Israel's army to the tent of Jael. He asked for water but she gave him warm milk and when the weary king went to sleep, she killed him with a hammer and tent peg.

You were not born to live a carnal existence with no purpose. How can He not be with us as we strive to fulfill His purpose with our lives.

Day 193 Is 47-49; Rom 8-9; Ps 97-99

Ps 99:8 "O Lord our God, Thou didst answer them; Thou were a forgiving God to them, and yet an avenger of their evil deeds."

Moses, Aaron and Samson were called by the Lord's name, but they were flawed like everyone else. So, the Lord punished their deeds.

Jesus said in Mt 26:41 "Watch and pray, lest you enter into temptation. The spirit indeed is willing, but the flesh is weak."

I Cor 3:11-15 "For no man can lay a foundation other than the one which is laid, which is Jesus Christ. Now if any man builds upon the foundation with gold, silver, precious stones, wood, hay straw, each man's work will become evident; for the day will show it, because it is to be revealed with fire; and the fire itself will test the quality of each man's work. If any man's work is burned up, he shall suffer loss; but he himself shall be saved, yet so as through fire."

Day 194 Is 50-52; Rom 10-11; Ps 100-102

The paintings of Jesus being crucified are very tame compared to the reality.

Is 50:6 His beard was torn out of His face so He was unrecognizable.

Is 52:14-15 "Just as many were astonished at Him, His appearance was marred more than any man, and His form more than the sons of men. Thus He will sprinkle many nations."

Jesus was beaten until His body was a bloody mass, the whips were made to cut into the flesh and tear pieces out. A crown of thorns was pressed down onto His head so that blood ran down to mingle on His cheeks.

Is 53:2-5 "…He has no stately form or majesty that we should look upon Him, nor appearance that we should be attracted to Him. He was despised and forsaken of men, a man of sorrows, and acquainted with grief; and like one from whom men hide their face, He was despised, and we did not esteem Him. Surely our griefs He Himself bore, and our sorrows He carried; yet we ourselves esteemed Him stricken, smitten of God, and afflicted. But He was pierced through for our transgressions, He was crushed for our iniquities; the chastening for our well-being fell upon Him, and by His scourging we are healed."

People know the crucifixion was bad, but our imagination can't really picture how horrible it was.

Day 195 Is 53-55; Rom 12-13; Ps 103-105

Rom 12:19-21 "Never take your own revenge, beloved, but leave room for the wrath of God for it is written, 'Vengeance is Mine, I will repay,' says the Lord. (Deut 32:35) But if your enemy is hungry, feed him, and if he is thirsty, give him a drink; for in so doing you will heap burning coals upon his head.' Do not be overcome by evil, but overcome evil with good."

I Peter 3:9 "To sum up, let all be harmonious, sympathetic, brotherly, kindhearted, and humble in spirit; not returning evil for evil or insult for insult, but giving a blessing instead; for you were called for the very purpose that you might inherit a blessing."

Is 54:1 & 13 "Shout for joy, O barren one, you who have borne no child; break forth into joyful shouting and cry aloud, you who have not travailed; for the sons of the desolate one will be more numerous than the sons of the married woman,' says the Lord."

Jesus shows us His great love by dying for us while were His enemies, that we may draw others to His love by loving them while they hate us, which produces offspring for us.

Day 196 Is 56-58; Rom 14-15; Ps 106-108

The Church used to have influence in the realm of government, businesses and personal lives. The non-churched had respect and knew that in the time of trouble they could get help. Your children needed school clothes, you couldn't get a job, your house burned down; the Church was there.

Satan with his principalities and powers, moved to weaken the Church causing government to take charity away from the Church through welfare programs including Social Security and they stole the hearts of the people, but the Church let it happen. We thought, "They don't need our help, they can get help elsewhere." Our hearts turned inward, outreach died, and our hearts became empty. There are many faithful pastors, but also many who only care about keeping up membership and fundraising, they are the Pharisees of today. Where does that lead us?

Is 56:10-11 "His watchmen are blind, they are ignorant; all of them are dumb dogs, unable to bark; dreamers lying down, who love to slumber, and the dogs are greedy, they are not satisfied. And they are shepherds who have no understanding; they have all turned to their own way, each one to his unjust gain, to the last one."

I enjoy church services and the corporate worship, but if we don't have a means to serve the unchurched our works are worthless.

Day 197 Is 59-61; Rom 16- I Cor 1; Ps 109-111

Is 60:1-3 "Arise, shine; for your light has come! And the glory of the Lord has risen upon you. For behold, the darkness will cover the earth, and deep darkness the peoples; but the Lord will rise upon you and His glory will appear upon you. And nations will come to your light, and kings to the brightness of you rising."

A small candle can hardly be seen in the daylight, but it is really revealed in the dark. The light of Jesus in us is shown in times of darkness. Darkness has been steadily moving over us inch by inch. Christianity has less influence than ever before in our history. Godless people are educating the next generation in humanism. Godless people are passing laws to take all liberty from us. The Church is responsible by being slack in our faith and allowing the oil of the Holy Spirit to run low. Light actually has to move away for darkness to be visible. Darkness cannot blot out light. It's time for a new move of God in our country.

Pr 29:2 "When the righteous increase, the people rejoice; but when a wicked man rules, people groan."

Day 198 Is 62-64; I Cor 2-3; Ps 112-114

Ps 112:1 & 4 "Praise the Lord! How blessed is the man who fears the Lord, who delights greatly in His commandments. Light arises in the darkness for the upright; he is gracious and compassionate and righteous." Jesus is the light of the world; from Genesis to Revelation, He is the Alpha and the Omega of light. Whatever happens in your life, God's light is there with you, because we are the children of light.

Everything in life is a cycle like summer and winter, joy and sorrow.

Ps 30:5 "For His anger is but for a moment, His favor is for a lifetime; weeping may last for a night, but a shout of joy comes in the morning."

I Thess 5:16-18 "Rejoice always, pray without ceasing, in everything give thanks, for this is God's will for you in Christ Jesus."

Joy does not depend on your circumstances, it is a choice. Sometimes it is easy and other times you have to just decide to look on God's view, trouble is temporary.

Day 199 Is 65-Jer 1; I Cor 4-5; Ps 115-117

Jeremiah was prophet in the days of Josiah, Jehoiakim and Zedekiah Kings of Judah

Jer 1:5-6 "Before I formed you in the womb I knew you; and before you were born I consecrated you; I appointed you a prophet to the nations.' Then said I: 'Alas, Lord God! Behold, I do not know how to speak, because I am a youth."

This is almost a universal answer to anything The Lord asks of us. We can find any number of really good reasons why we are not the one for the job. Moses had a speech problem, but God used him. I wish I could always give the answer of Isaiah when I hear God's voice.

Is 6:8 "Then I heard the voice of the Lord, Saying: 'Whom shall I send, and who will go for Us?' Then I said, 'Here I am! Send me."

Isaiah did ask how long. Israel was to be punished again, until the land was desolate and would stay desolate until their return from Babylon.

Day 200 Jer 2-4; I Cor 6-7; Ps 118-120

Jer 2:2-3 "Go and proclaim in the ears of Jerusalem, saying, 'Thus says the Lord: 'I remember concerning you, the devotion of your youth, the love of your betrothals, your following after Me in the wilderness, through a land not sown. Israel was holy to the Lord, the first of His harvest; all who ate of it became guilty; evil came upon them,' declares the Lord."

When I read Exodus, I don't see a lot of faithfulness, but I have to remember that this reading took us through Exodus in 20 days. All that murmuring and complaining which seemed constant took place over a 40 year period (although I'm sure we read only a small part of all their grumbling).

The wilderness was a place of trying and testing and it is clear here that the Lord remembered it fondly.

We can be thankful that He removes our sin far from us when we repent.

Is 43:25 "I, even I, am the one who wipes out your transgressions for My own sake; and I will not remember your sins."

Day 201 Jer 5-7; I Cor 8-9; Ps 121-123

Jer 4:1-2 "If you will return, O Israel', declares the Lord, 'Then you should return to Me. And if you will put away your detested things from My presence, and will not waver, and you will swear, 'As the Lord lives, in truth, in justice, and in righteousness; then the nations will bless themselves in Him, and in Him they will glory."

Jer 5:3 & 10 "O Lord, do not Thine eyes look for truth? Thou hast smitten them, but they did not weaken, Thou hast consumed them, but they refused to take correction. They have made their faces harder than rock; they have refused to repent." "Go up through her vine rows and destroy, but do not execute a complete destruction; …"

The Lord saved a remnant.

I K 19:10 When Elijah said: "....the sons of Israel have forsaken Thy covenant, torn down Thine altars, and killed Thy prophets with the sword, I alone am left, and they seek my life." The Lord answered, "I have kept for Myself seven thousand men who have not bowed the knee to Baal."

II K 19:30-31 "And the surviving remnant of the house of Judah shall again take root downward and bear fruit upward For out of Jerusalem shall go forth a remnant, and out of Mount Zion survivors. The zeal of the Lord shall perform this."

The Lord does not need a huge army, the willing few are greater.

Day 202 Jer 8-10; I Cor 10-11; Ps 124-126

Ps 125:1-3 "Those who trust in the Lord are like Mount Zion, which cannot be moved, but abides forever. As the mountains surround Jerusalem, so the Lord surrounds His people from this time forth and forever."

If we sin, it is because we decide to sin. The Lord has put His protection around us and the only way to sin is move away from Him.

There was a story of an elderly couple riding in their car and the woman noticing a young couple with the girl scrunched up against the young man as He drove by. She said wistfully," we used to ride around like that." And her husband answered, "I didn't move." In the exciting days of first knowing the Lord, we can't get enough of His presence, but the relationship has to mature. Then we have a less giddy emotion as we grow into a deeper love, but if you are not as close to the Lord as you used to be, you know who moved. Meditate on His Word and feed your soul.

I Cor 10:13 "No temptation has overtaken you except such as is common to man but God is faithful, who will not allow you to be tempted beyond what you are able, but with the temptation will also make a way of escape, that you may be able to bear it."

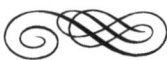

Day 203 Jer 11-13; I Cor 12-13; Ps 127-129

I Cor 12:4 & 7-11 "There are varieties of gifts, but the same Spirit. But to each one is given the manifestation of the Spirit for the common good. For to one is given the word of wisdom through the Spirit, and to another the word of knowledge according to the same Spirit; to another faith by the same Spirit, and to another gifts of healing by the one Spirit, and to another the effecting of miracles, and to another prophecy, and to another the distinguishing of spirits, to another various kinds of tongues, and to another the interpretation of tongues. But one and the same Spirit works all these things, distributing to each one individually just as He will."

Gal 5:22 "But the fruit of the Spirit is love, joy, peace, patience, kindness, goodness, faithfulness, gentleness, self-control, against such there is no law."

All these gifts and fruits weave together a positive tapestry of our lives that is pleasing to the Lord. The 9 gifts are for specific ministry but the 9 fruits are for everyone to produce in abundance, and fruit reproduces.

Day 204 Jer 14-16; I Cor 14-15; Ps 130-132

A great drought had come on Jerusalem. The cisterns were empty and the earth produced no grass.

Jeremiah calls out to the Lord for rain.

Jer 14:7 & 9 "Although our iniquities testify against us, O Lord, act for Thy name's sake! Truly our apostates have been many, we have sinned against Thee. Why art Thou like a man dismayed. Like a mighty man who cannot save? Yet Thou art in our midst, O Lord. And we are called by Thy name; do not forsake us!"

In Deuteronomy, there is a litany of blessings and curses.

De 28:23-24 "And the heavens which are over your head shall be bronze, and the earth which is under you shall be iron. The Lord will make the rain of your land to powder and dust; from heaven it shall come down on you until you are destroyed." Jeremiah hit on the very thing which kept God from wiping out all the descendants of Jacob.

The first was His plan to have Messiah born in the line of Judah and the second was the reproach of all the nations around them who would say that the God of Israel was too weak to save them.

Day 205 Jer 17-19; I Cor 16- II Cor 1; Ps 133-135

Jer 18: 3-4 "Then I went down to the potter's house, and there he was, making something at the wheel.

But the vessel that he was making of clay was spoiled in the hand of the potter; so he remade it into another vessel, as it pleased the potter to make."

Is 64:8 "But now, O Lord, Thou art our Father, we are the clay, and Thou are our potter: and all of us are the work of Thy hand."

Eph 2:10 "For we are His workmanship created in Christ Jesus for good works, which God prepared beforehand that we should walk in them."

Ecclesiastes 9:10 "Whatever your hand finds to do, verily, do it with your might;"

Everyone has a purpose in God and many never know it. Think about what pleases you that is a benefit to others and to God, you may be astonished at what you find.

Day 206 Jer 20-22; II Cor 2-3; Ps 136-138

Jer 1:10 "See, I have appointed you this day over the nations and over the kingdoms, to pluck up and to break down, to destroy and to overthrow, to build and to plant."

Like a garden that is so overgrown with weeds, all you can do is plow it up and start fresh again. No one liked Jeremiah's words from the Lord, friends deserted him.

Jer 20:9-13 "But if I say, 'I will not remember Him Or speak anymore in His name,' Then in my heart it becomes like a burning fire shut up in my bones; and I am weary of holding it in, and I cannot endure it.

For I have heard the whispering of many, terror on every side! Denounce him; yes, let us denounce him!' All my trusted friends, watching for my fall, say: 'Perhaps he will be deceived, so that we may prevail against him.' But the Lord is with me like a dread champion; therefore my persecutors will stumble and not prevail. They will be utterly ashamed, because they have failed, with an everlasting disgrace that will not be forgotten. Yet, O Lord of hosts, Thou who dost test the righteous, who seest the mind and the heart; let me see Thy vengeance on them; for to Thee I have set forth my cause, sing to the Lord, praise the Lord! For He has delivered the soul of the needy one from the hand of the evildoers."

Jeremiah went from woe, to trust, to praise; obedience brings its own reward.

Day 207 Jer 23-25; II Cor 4-5; Ps 139-141

II Cor 5:17 "Therefore if any man is in Christ, he is a new creature; old things have passed away; behold new things have come."

Eph 2:4-5 "But God, being rich in mercy, because of His great love with which He loved us, even when we were dead in trespasses, made us alive together with Christ (by grace you have been saved),"

Eph 2:13-18 "But now in Christ Jesus you who formerly were far off have been brought near by the blood of Christ. For He Himself is our peace, who made both groups into one, and broke down the barrier of the dividing wall, by abolishing in His flesh the enmity, which is the law of commandments contained in ordinances, that in Himself He might make the two into one new man, thus establishing peace, and might reconcile them both in one body to God through the cross, by it having put to death the enmity. And He came and preached peace to you who were far away, and peace to those who were near; for through Him we both have our access in one Spirit to the Father."

We are not just living flesh now, but are a living spirit because we have been joined to Him, we were dead and now we are alive. Sometimes as I am waking up, I hear my spirit singing and now and then when I'm awake, worship rising up from that spirit that was made alive in me.

Day 208 Jer 26-28; II Cor 6-7; Ps 142-144

II Cor 6:14 & 16 "Do not be bound together with unbelievers; for what partnership have righteousness with lawlessness, or what fellowship has light with darkness? Or what agreement has the temple of God with idols? For we are the temple of the living God; …."

We are surrounded by unbelievers, working beside them and co-operating with them in our jobs. We cannot separate ourselves from the unsaved and I don't think God expects or even wants us to do so. Jesus is the light of the world and we are like His moon, reflecting the light of the son. We are His witnesses to a world of darkness and the only light that the lost sees may be you.

I Tim 2:1-4 "First of all, then, I urge that entreaties and prayers, petitions and thanksgivings be made on behalf of all men, for kings and all who are in authority, in order that we may lead a tranquil and quiet life in all godliness and dignity. This is good and acceptable in the sight of God our Savior, who desires all men to be saved and to come to the knowledge of the truth."

Day 209 Jer 29-31; II Cor 8-9; Ps 145-147

Kings come and go. This king is good and that king is evil. One thing that never changed was that the people continued to worship idols. God is very patient, but don't test Him beyond His limits. Finally, He spoke to them through His prophet to tell them they were going to be taken into slavery.

Jer 29:10 "For thus says the Lord: 'When seventy years have been completed for Babylon, I will visit you and fulfill My good word to you, to bring you back to this place." In seventy years an entire new generation of adults will be in leadership positions.

In this day and age idol worship seems to have gone out of fashion, we are too intelligent to bow down to ugly creatures made of wood and stone, or is Satan just more subtle now? An idol is that thing that stands between you and the will of God for you; empty pastimes, sports, television, computer games, reading that does not edify. And that root of all evil, the love of money for its own sake and which pays for all those pleasures. Idolatry is all around us, but it wears a very pleasant mask.

Day 210 Jer 32-34; II Cor 10-11; Ps 148-150

II Cor 10:3-5 "For though we walk in the flesh, we do not war according to flesh, for the weapons of our warfare are not of flesh but divinely powerful for the destruction of fortresses. We are destroying speculations and every lofty thing raised up against the knowledge of God, and we are taking every thought captive to the obedience of Christ,"

Mt 22:36-40 Jesus was tested by the Pharisees, they asked, "Teacher which is the great commandment in the law?' Jesus said to him, 'You shall love the Lord your God with all your heart, with all your soul, and with all your mind. This is the great and foremost commandment. And the second is like it, you shall love your neighbor as yourself,' 'On these two commandments depend the whole Law and the Prophets."

Holding onto pain will poison your soul, because God's Law is love.

I Peter 4:8 "Above all, keep fervent in your love for one another, because love will cover a multitude of sins."

Day 211 Jer 35-37; II Cor 12-13; Ps 1-3

There are magazines devoted to famous people in entertainment and their fans avidly read about their favorite stars. No matter how many articles they read, all they can see is the false face of their idol.

Ps 1 If we want to be blessed by the Lord, we first have to know Him AND know about Him. Don't take directions from the ungodly; their roadmap will take you to a dead-end in the swamp surrounded by gators.

Take delight in the Lord and His Law. Meditating in His Law will drive our roots deep to hold us firm. When the storms of life hit us, our roots will not be pulled up nor will our fruit be swept away. As the wind drives the chaff away, the lost will still be shouting back at us the directions to the swamp. We want to stand firm in the judgment and in the congregation of the righteous. There is no greater joy than being in the Lord's presence.

Day 212 Jer 38-40; Gal 1-2; Ps 4-6

The prophecies of Jeremiah were not accepted by the rich and powerful of Jerusalem.

Jer 38:2 "Thus says the Lord: 'He who stays in this city will die by the sword and by famine, and by pestilence, but he who goes out to the Chaldeans will live and have his own life as booty and stay alive." The princes wanted to put Jeremiah to death, so they put him in a pit where it was mire but no drinking water. Ebed-Melech, an Ethiopian eunuch, who was a servant to King Zedekiah asked for the life of Jeremiah. After Jeremiah was pulled up, Zedekiah asked again for the Word of the Lord.

Jer 38:17 "...Thus says the Lord God of hosts, the God of Israel: 'If you will indeed go out to the officers of the king of Babylon, then you will live, this city will not be burned with fire, and you and your household will survive."

Instead of obeying the Lord, the king fled and was caught by the Chaldeans, his sons and nobles were killed in front of Him before they put out his eyes and took him prisoner. Jerusalem was burned. Proverbs 3:5-6 "Trust in the Lord with all heart, and do not lean on your own understanding; in all your ways acknowledge Him, and He will make your paths straight."

After asking for the Lord's directions, King Zedekiah went his own way.

Day 213 Jer 41-43; Gal 3-4; Ps 7-9

Gal 4:19 "My children, with whom I am again in labor until Christ is formed in you."

We have to labor hard and travail long for the soul of the rebel. We are fighting the desires of their flesh, people enjoy their sins and rebellion comes as natural as breathing. We are fighting the devil, who was subtle enough to deceive Eve. She saw God face to face. And yet the devil made sin look so delicious that she ignored the one thing that the Lord had withheld from her.

I prayed for my grandson until he accepted the Lord and was baptized. When he became a teenager, I had to go back to the labor and I am still in labor to this day. This young man has visited the pleasures of sin and the second travail is longer and harder than the first and is still ongoing.

John 16:21 "Whenever a woman is in travail she has sorrow, because her hour has come; but when she gives birth to the child, she remembers the anguish no more, for joy that a child has been born into the world."

Day 214 Jer 44-46; Gal 5-6; Ps 10-12

Gen 37:23-28 The Lord sent Joseph into Egypt and then used famine to bring the rest of the family of Jacob to live there.

Another Joseph, the husband of Mary was told to take Jesus and Mary into Egypt when Herod was determined to kill the new king.

Mt 2:13 & 15 …"that what was spoken by the Lord through the prophet might be fulfilled, saying, 'Out Egypt did I call My Son.'"

Jeremiah warned that this time God's plan was definitely not Egypt, it was Babylon. The Lord through Jeremiah warned the people to surrender to the Chaldeans and they would live.

Jer 44:12 "And I will take the remnant of Judah who have set their faces to go into the land of Egypt to dwell there, and they shall all be consumed and fall in the land of Egypt. They shall be consumed by the sword and by famine. They shall die, from the least to the greatest, by the sword and by the famine; and they shall be an oath, an astonishment, a curse and a reproach!"

Day 212 King Zedekiah refused the word of the Lord to surrender and was killed.

The Lord's plan for us changes from season to season, from week to week. Like a surfer has to catch the right wave, we need to watch and pray that we don't miss our wave.

Day 215 Jer 47-49; Eph 1-2; Ps 13-15

Jer 48:10 "Cursed be the one who does the Lord's work negligently, and cursed be the one who restrains his sword from blood"

I Sam 15:3 & 9 "Now go and attack Amalek, and utterly destroy all that he has, and do not spare him; but put to death both man and woman, child and infant, ox and sheep, camel and donkey. But Saul and the people spared Agag and the best of the sheep, the oxen, the fatlings, the lambs, and all that was good, and were not willing to destroy them utterly; …."

Saul thought he was wiser than God to discern what was good. Do we follow our own thoughts instead of God's leading? Now the Lord's sword which is the Word of God is given to us to wield at His demand. Ps 119:11 "Thy word I have treasured in my heart, that I may not sin against Thee." If we have stored His word in our hearts, the opportunity will come to release His words instead of our words.

Heb 4:12-13 "For the word of God is living and active, and sharper than any two-edged sword, piercing as far as the division of soul and spirit, of both joints and marrow, and able to judge the thoughts and intentions of the heart. And there is no creature hidden from His sight, but all things are open and laid bare to the eyes of Him with whom we have to do.."

Day 216 Jer 50-52; Eph 3-4; Ps 16-18

Eph 3:8-12 "To me, the very least of all the saints, this grace was given, to preach to the Gentiles the unfathomable riches of Christ, and to bring to light what is the administration of the mystery which for ages has been hidden in God, who created all things; in order that the manifold wisdom of God might now be made known through the church to the rulers and the authorities in the heavenly places. This was in accordance with the eternal purpose which He carried out in Christ Jesus our Lord, in whom we have boldness and confident access through faith in Him."

Who are these powers and principalities in the heavenly places? It could be angels and demons. When the devil and his angels (who became demons) rebelled against God and had to be thrown out of Heaven, were others watching? Many have speculated about life on other planets and I've wondered if there were life out there and they had not sinned, the earth is a good lesson to stay faithful to God. Whoever they are they can see us and we are privileged to reveal the mysteries of God to them. Our sight is limited by sin but in the spirit world there is no distance.

Day 217 Lam 1-3; Eph 5-6; Ps 19-21

Is 59:15-18 "...Now the Lord saw, and it was displeasing in His sight that there was no justice. And he saw that there was no man, and was astonished that there was no one to intercede; then His own arm brought salvation to Him; and His righteousness like a breastplate, and a helmet of salvation on His head; and He put on garments of vengeance for clothing, and wrapped himself with zeal as a mantle. According to their deeds, so He will repay, wrath to His adversaries, recompense to His enemies; to the coastlands He will make recompense."

This shows the Lord bringing salvation and justice, but in the church age that responsibility is given to us.

Eph 6:10 "Finally, be strong in the Lord and in the strength of His might. Put on the full armor of God, that you may be able to stand firm against the schemes of the devil. For our struggle is not against flesh and blood, but against the rulers, against the powers, against the world forces of this darkness, against the spiritual forces of wickedness in the heavenly places."

And then He gave us weapons and protection for battle, offense and defense.

Day 218 Lam 4-Ezek 1; Phil 1-2; Ps 22-24

Ezekiel began to prophecy in the 5th year of the captivity of King Jehoiachin

Phil 2:1-5 "If therefore there is any encouragement in Christ, if there is any consolation of love, if there is any fellowship of the Spirit, if any affection and compassion, make my joy complete by being of the same mind, maintaining the same love, united in spirit, intent on one purpose. Do nothing from selfishness or empty conceit, but with humility of mind let each of you regard one another as more important than himself; do not merely look out for your personal interests, but also for the interests of others. Have this attitude in yourselves which was also in Christ Jesus,"

Mt 5:43-45 "You have heard that it was said, 'You shall love your neighbor and hate your enemy.' But I say to you, love your enemies, bless those who curse you, and pray for those who persecute you in order that you may be sons of your Father who is in heaven,"

Day 219 Ezek 2-4; Phil 3-4; Ps 25-27

Ez 3:17-19 "Son of man, I have appointed you a watchman to the house of Israel; whenever you hear a word from My mouth, warn them from Me. "When I say to the wicked, 'You shall surely die'; and you do not warn him or speak out to warn the wicked from his wicked way that he may live, that wicked man shall die in his iniquity, but his blood I will require at your hand. Yet if you have warned the wicked, and he does not turn from his wickedness or from his wicked way, he shall die in his iniquity; but you have delivered yourself."

We are surrounded by unsaved people, what are we supposed to do? Some will say we live a life of example, that's true, without an example our words are tainted, but without words our example is not enough. Look for people who need a prayer said on their behalf.

Peter 3:15 "...Always being ready to make a defense to every one who asks you to give an account for the hope that is in you, yet with gentleness and reverence;"

Paul and the other early leaders didn't wait for people to notice them, they turned their world upside down. The early church were shouted down, beaten, killed. But when the unsaved ignore us, we say,

"Oh well, there's nothing I can do." We need a more aggressive plan. The first step is prayer, which prepares the ground for seed and prepares us to be less timid.

Day 220 Ezek 5-7; Col 1-2; Ps 28-30

Col 1:10 "so that you may walk in a manner worthy of the Lord, to please Him in all respects, bearing fruit in every good work and increasing in the knowledge of God;"

The Lord wants a generous people, generous with time as well as tithes and offerings. One of the ministries in I Cor 12:28, is helps. I met a woman who wasn't able to drive herself to go shopping but refused to allow her daughter or friends to take her because she didn't want to be a burden. She always had believed it was more blessed to give than to receive (she told me so), but didn't see that she was keeping a blessing from others by refusing help. Pride takes many forms. There is little more humbling than growing old and having to depend on help with all the things that you never gave a thought to when you were young. Allow others to be blessed through you, sometimes giving help and sometimes by gracefully receiving it.

Day 221 Ezek 8-10; Col 3-4; Ps 31-33

Ps 30:1 & 5 & 11-12 "I will extol Thee, O Lord, for Thou hast lifted me up, and hast not let my foes rejoice over me. Weeping may endure for a night, but a shout of joy comes in the morning. Thou hast turned for me my mourning into dancing; Thou hast loosed my sackcloth and girded me with gladness; that my soul may sing praise to Thee and not be silent. O Lord my God, I will give thanks to Thee forever."

He has blessed us so much; we cannot be silent as we glory in His mercy. We can't even call ourselves unworthy of His sacrifice because He says we are worth everything He suffered.

The enemy had knocked us down and had his foot on our head and we were helpless, but Jesus lifted us up.

Col 3:1 & 8 "If then you were raised up with Christ, keep seeking the things above, where Christ is seated at the right hand of God. But now you also put these all aside: anger, wrath, malice, slander, and abusive speech from your mouth."

Day 222 Ezek 11-13; I Thess 1-2; Ps 34-36

Ez 11:15 & 17-20 "Son of man, your brethren, your relatives, your fellow exiles, and the whole house of Israel, all of them, are those to whom the inhabitants of Jerusalem have said, 'Go far from the Lord; this land has been given us as a possession.'" "Therefore say, 'Thus says the Lord God, 'I shall gather you from the peoples and assemble you out of the countries among which you have been scattered, and I shall give you the land of Israel. When they come there, they will remove all its detestable things and all its abominations from it. And I shall give them one heart, and shall put a new spirit within them. And I shall take the heart of stone out of their flesh and give them a heart of flesh, that they may walk in My statutes and keep My ordinances, and do them. Then they will be My people, and I shall be their God."

For those who think God is done with Israel this shows us they are still part of His agenda. There is no other way to explain why Israel is a nation again, they were gone, they were scattered and now the chosen remnant have been gathered back again. Bible scholars of the early 1900's said Israel was over and done with, yet in 1948, they became a nation again. He is able to fulfill His promises.

Day 223 Ezek 14-16; I Thess 3-4; Ps 37-39

Ez 14 Idols are not only gruesome statues we sit in front of and bow down to, they are in the heart. The Amplified Bible in verse 4 lists objects of idolatry as self-will and unsubmissiveness. Worship begins in the heart whether it is the Lord or anything that is not the Lord. All mankind has a need to worship and we will worship something. It is as natural as blinking your eyes and as unconscious. Look around and make a list of the things that are using most of your time. Work at any job and it takes a lot of your time and caring for our families and their needs takes another big chunk. But if we are alert to watch ourselves we will find so much stuff that does nothing to enhance our lives or bring us closer to God.

He will convict us if we don't make our hearts so hard and our ears so dull that we cannot see or hear.

Day 224 Ezek 17-19; I Thess 5-II Thess 1; Ps 40-42

Ps 40:2-3 "He brought me up out of a pit of destruction, out of the miry clay: and He set my feet upon a rock making my footsteps firm. And He put a new song in my mouth a song of praise to our God; many will see and fear, and will trust in the Lord."

Our testimony is powerful to turn the lost to God, but it needs to be a positive testimony, glorifying God with our praise. Then, they need to see the results, how you are changed. The fruit of the Spirit will begin to manifest itself very quickly and people are drawn to His sweet fruit, but not to sour grapes. Let your newfound joy and peace be in full display. All believers must have fruit but our purpose in the Lord is unique to us.

II Cor 4:7 "But we have this treasure in earthen vessels, that the surpassing greatness of the power may be of God and not from ourselves;"

He is the potter and makes pots for many different purposes but all are useful to Him. The process of turning clay into something useful takes a considerable time, dug up, cleaned, purified and shaped, then when it comes into the fire it may break. Strength comes from His Word and drawing near to Him.

Day 225 Ezek 20-22; II Thess 2-3; Ps 43-45

Ez 22:30 "And I searched for a man among them who should build up the wall and stand in the gap before Me for the land, that I should not destroy it; but I found no one."

The Lord continually looks for an intercessor to stand between judgment and the guilty. Men rebelled against Moses as leader, and God judged them.

Num 16:32 "and the earth opened its mouth and swallowed them up, and their households and all the men who belonged to Korah, with their possessions.

Num 16:41 & 46-48 "But on the next day all the congregation of the sons of Israel grumbled against Moses and Aaron, saying 'You are the ones who have caused the death of the Lord's people. And Moses said to Aaron, 'Take a censer and put fire in it from the altar, and lay incense on it, and bring it quickly to the congregation and made an atonement for them; for wrath has gone forth from the Lord, the plague has begun.' Then Aaron took it as Moses had spoken, and ran into the midst of the assembly; for behold the plague had begun among the people. So he put on the incense and made atonement for the people.

And he took his stand between the dead and the living; so that the plague was stopped."

Jesus is the atonement for sin, but we have a part.

II Cor 5:18 "Now all things are from God, who reconciled us to Himself through Jesus Christ, and gave us the ministry of reconciliation.

Day 226 Ezek 23-25; I Tim 1-2; Ps 46-48

I Tim 2:8 "Therefore I want the men in every place to pray, lifting up holy hands, without wrath and doubting;"

The church today is a mere shadow of the power and unity of the early church. They met daily and spent many hours in prayer. The church was being hunted and imprisoned or stoned to death, so it was serious business. Prayer is communion, requesting, praising, thanking, making confession and being in His presence.

Jesus told them to pray for: "Thy kingdom come, Thy will be done; that you may not enter into temptation; at all times they ought to pray and not lose heart. Watch and pray always that you might have the strength to escape all these things that will come to pass, and to stand before the Son of Man."

(Also read, Mt 6:10; Mt 26:41; Luke 18:1; Luke 21:16.)

James 4:3 & 5:16 "You ask and do not receive, because you ask with wrong motives, so that you may spend it on your pleasures. Therefore confess your sins to one another, and pray for one another, so that you may be healed. The effective, fervent prayer of a righteous man can accomplish much."

Day 227 Ezek 26-28; I Tim 3-4; Ps 49-51

This is a description of Lucifer which means angel of light.

Ez 28:12-17 "...You had the seal of perfection, full of wisdom and perfect in beauty, you were in Eden, the garden of God; ….. You were the anointed cherub who covers; I placed you there. You were on the holy mountain of God; you walked in the midst of fiery stones. You were perfect in your ways from the day you were created, till iniquity was found in you….. Your heart was lifted up because of your beauty; you corrupted your wisdom by reason of your splendor; I cast you to the ground, I laid you before kings, that they might gaze at you."

It seems that there were people on the earth when Satan was cast down, before Adam was created.

Mt 4:8-9 Satan owns the kingdoms of the world and offered to give them to Jesus in exchange for His worship, but the god of this world was the loser in that contest.

Day 228 Ezek 29-31; I Tim 5-6; Ps 52-54

Deut 6:13-15 & 24 "You shall fear only the Lord your God; and you shall worship Him, and swear by His name. You shall not follow other gods, the gods of the peoples who surround you, for the Lord your God in the midst of you is a jealous God; ….So the Lord commanded us to observe all these statutes, to fear the Lord our God, for our good always, and for our survival as it is today."

What keeps us from talking to friends about their need to be saved? Fear! What keeps us silent in family gatherings about the things of the Lord? Fear! Who said, you can't talk about religion and politics in any group? The devil did, that's who. The author of this fear is the devil. We need to look carefully at any fear that is not fear of the Lord. He is the father who loves us always. Our sin hurts Him just as earthly parents hurt when their children seek fun but find trouble. God's people can have fun but finding a habit of joy is very important so we don't have to be constant thrill seekers.

Ps 16:8-11 "I have set the Lord continually before me; because He is at my right hand, I shall not be shaken. Therefore my heart is glad and my glory rejoices; my flesh also will dwell securely. For Thou wilt not abandon my soul in Sheol, neither wilt Thou allow Thy Holy One to undergo decay. Thou wilt make known to me the path of life; in Thy presence is fullness of joy; in Thy right hand there are pleasures forever.

Day 229 Ezek 32-34; II Tim 1-2; Ps 55-57

Ez 33:1-7 "And the word of the Lord came to me saying, 'Son of man speak to the sons of your people and say to them, 'If I bring a sword upon a land, and the people of the land take one man from among them and make him their watchman; and he sees the sword coming upon the land, and he blows on the trumpet and warns the people, then he who hears the sound of the trumpet and does not take warning, and a sword comes and takes him away, his blood will be on his own head. He heard the sound of the trumpet, but did not take warning; his blood will be on himself. But had he taken warning, he would have delivered his life. But if the watchman sees the sword coming and does not blow the trumpet, and the people are not warned, and a sword comes and takes a person from them, he is taken away in his iniquity; but his blood I will require from the watchman's hand. Now as for you, son of man: I have appointed you a watchman"

This is repeating the same principle as in Ezekiel chapter 3 and since God said it twice, I will too.

People are in the dark but don't know where the switch is, they can't turn it on without our help.

Luke 4:18 (Is 61:1) "The Spirit of the Lord is upon Me, because He anointed Me to preach the gospel to the poor; He has sent Me to proclaim release to the captives and recovery of sight to the blind, to set free those who are downtrodden,"

Day 230 Ezek 35-37; II Tim 3-4; Ps 58-60; Pr 1

Ez 36:17-28 "Son of man, when the house of Israel was living in their own land, they defiled it by their ways and their deeds; …..Therefore I poured out My wrath on them for the blood which they had shed on the land, because they had defiled it with their idols. Also I scattered them among the nations, and they were dispersed throughout the lands; according to their ways I judged them. But I had concern for My holy name,… Therefore say to the house of Israel, Thus says the Lord God, It is not for your sake, but for My holy name,….For I will take you from among the nations, gather you out of all the lands, and bring you into your own land. Then I will sprinkle clean water on you, and you will be clean; …I will give you a new heart and put a new spirit within you. … so you will be My people."

Rom 11:26 & 29 By this promise Paul knew the Lord had not forgotten Israel and could say with confidence, "..all Israel will be saved" and "the gifts and the calling of God are irrevocable."

Day 231 Ezek 38-40; Titus 1-2; Ps 61-63; Pr 2

Pr 2:10-12 "For wisdom enters your heart, and knowledge will be pleasant to your soul, discretion will guard you, understanding will watch over you, to deliver you from the way of evil, from the man who speaks perverse things."

The man who speaks perverse things is one who rejects the truth.

Rom 1:18-20 "For the wrath of God is revealed from heaven against all ungodliness and unrighteousness of men, who suppress the truth in unrighteousness, because that which is known about God is evident to them. For since the creation of the world His invisible attributes, His eternal power and divine nature, have been clearly seen, being understood through what has been made, so that they are without excuse,"

People who reject the truth will believe lies and because Jesus is the light of the world, darkness envelopes those who reject the Light.

II Cor 4:3-4 "And even if our gospel is veiled, it is veiled to those who are perishing, in whose case the god of this world has blinded the minds …"

Pray for light to break through the darkness of the mind of your unsaved loved ones.

Day 232 Ezek 41-43; Titus 3-Philem; Ps 64-66; Pr 3

Pr 3:11-12 "My son, do not reject the discipline of the Lord, or loathe His reproof, for whom the Lord loves He reproves, even as a father, the son in whom he delights."

In the flesh, I hate to be corrected; we like to think we are more spiritual than some others we see. One day I was kneeling in my garden pulling weeds and mulling over my hurt feelings and realized that I had not felt the Lord's presence for a long while. The Lord pulled me up and showed me the grudge I was holding. I sat back and said, "Lord, I thought I had learned to forgive." Immediately I heard a mother's voice inside my head speaking to her little child, "I've told you over and over and over and over…." The Lord reminded me that learning a lesson doesn't mean that we will always make the right decision the next time temptation comes around. Like little children we are likely to follow instinct instead of Him and have to be taught over and over and over and over.

Jesus called us His little children and too often we have to learn by repetition.

Day 233 Ezek 44-46; Heb 1-2; Ps 67-69; Pr 4

Heb 1:13-14 "But to which of the angels has He ever said: 'Sit at My right hand, until I make Thine enemies a footstool for Thy feet?' Are they not all ministering spirits sent out to render service for the sake of those who will inherit salvation?"

A lot of nonsense is written today about angels, there is no mention in the scripture of everyone or anyone having a guardian angel. Many have a false impression of who they are.

Angels are non-gendered (Mt 22:30) but in the Bible, every time an angel appears to men they are in the form of a man often holding a huge sword.

Num 22:31 "Then the Lord opened the eyes of Balaam, and he saw the angel of the Lord standing in the way with His drawn sword in His Hand; and he bowed all the way to the ground."

When people die they do not become angels. Angels were created by God and are separate beings and angels are not our servants with the power to answer our prayers. They are servants of the Most High God! If they help us, it is because He sent them.

Day 234 Ezek 47-Dan 1; Heb 3-4; Ps 70-72; Pr 5

Daniel had visions during the captivity in Babylon

Heb 3:8-11 "Do not harden your hearts as when they provoked Me, as in the day of trial in the wilderness, where your fathers tried Me by testing Me, and saw My works for forty years. Therefore I was angry with this generation, and said, 'They always go astray in their heart; and they did not know My ways; as I swore in My wrath, they shall not enter My Rest."

The Lord's Rest is rest from our enemies, they have been defeated, not by our power, but by the completed work of Jesus Christ. The people of Israel never did completely clear the land of the idolatrous people. The enemy continued to be a snare to them.

Heb 4:8-11 "For if Joshua had given them rest, He would not have spoken of another day after that.

There remains therefore a Sabbath rest for the people of God. For the one who has entered His Rest has himself also rested from his works as God did from His. Let us therefore be diligent to enter that rest, lest anyone fall through following to the same example of disobedience."

That is the Lord's Rest.

Day 235 Dan 2-4; Heb 5-6; Ps 73-75; Pr 6

Dan 3:28 Nebuchadnezzar after seeing the miracle of men thrown into a furnace and coming out unharmed, gave acknowledgement to the Lord. But, he was still an arrogant unbeliever. Then the Lord sent the king another vision.

Dan 4:10-16 He saw a great tree that covered the earth. Daniel revealed that the tree was Nebuchadnezzar and judgment was decreed that the king would become like a beast. Did the king repent and do his best to live up to God's desire for him? No.

Dan 4:29-31 "Twelve months later he was walking on the roof of the royal palace of Babylon. The king reflected and said, 'Is this not Babylon the great which I myself have built as a royal residence by the might of my power and for the glory of my majesty?' While the word was in the king's mouth, a voice came from heaven saying, 'King Nebuchadnezzar, to you it is declared: sovereignty has been removed from you, the kingdom has departed from you!"

Nebuchadnezzar had 12 months warning and ignored it, so he spent 7 years eating grass and living in the open like an ox.

Dan 4:34 "But at the end of that period I, Nebuchadnezzar, raised my eyes toward heaven, and my reason returned to me; and I blessed the Most High and praised and honored Him who lives forever; …."

Could he have saved himself 7 years if he had humbled himself before the Lord sooner? I believe so.

Day 236 Dan 5-7; Heb 7-8; Ps 76-78; Pr 7

All the Law given to Moses was an act of love. Just as we tell our little children not to touch the hot stove and don't run into the street. Love attempts to protect from the folly of sin. The commandments actually revealed to the people the sinful impulses they had from the youngest to the oldest.

Heb 8:5-7 "…Moses was warned by God when he was about to erect the tabernacle; for, 'See,' He says, that you make all things according to the pattern which was shown you on the mountain.' But now He has obtained a more excellent ministry, by as much as He is also the mediator of a better covenant, which has been enacted on better promises. For if that first covenant had been faultless, there would have been no occasion sought for a second."

II Cor 3:5-8 "…our adequacy is from God, who also made us adequate as servants of a new covenant, but of the Spirit; for the letter kills, but the Spirit gives life. But if the ministry of death, in letters engraved on stones, came with glory, so that the sons of Israel could not look intently at the face of Moses because of the glory of his face, fading as it was, how shall the ministry of the Spirit fail to be even more with glory?"

Day 237 Dan 8-10; Heb 9-10; Ps 79-81; Pr 8

Many have written about the visions of the latter days, so I have purposely not repeated their studies.

But, this picture of Daniel praying is very revealing.

Dan 10:2-3 "In those days I, Daniel, was mourning three entire weeks. I did not eat any tasty food, nor did meat or wine enter my mouth, nor did I use any ointment at all, until the entire three weeks were completed."

Daniel prayed for three weeks and when the angel came, he explained the delay. "…from the first day that you set your heart to understanding this and on humbling yourself before your God, your words were heard; and I have come in response to your words. But the prince of the kingdom of Persia withstood me twenty-one days; then behold, Michael, one of the chief princes, came to help me, for I had been left alone there with the kings of Persia."

The kings of Persia are the demons that are over that territory. The arch angels that we are told about are Gabriel, Michael and Lucifer, each having angelic forces in their command. Earthly armies are based on this chain of command system. Lucifer or Satan has his forces deployed and strong demons are responsible for controlling the area of false religions. If Daniel, God's prophet had to pray for three weeks, this shows us that we can't throw a few words into space and expect an instantaneous answer.

Dig in, hang on and don't give up until the answer comes.

Day 238 Dan 11-Hos 1; Heb 11-12; Ps 82-84; Pr 9

Hosea prophesied in the days of Uzziah, Jotham, Ahaz and Hezekiah kings of Judah

Ps 84:10 "For a day in Thy courts is better than a thousand. I had rather be a doorkeeper in the house of my God than dwell in the tents of wickedness." (KJV)

Before anyone was allowed to enter the Lord's house, the doorkeeper washed their feet.

John 10:7 "Jesus therefore said to them again, 'Truly, truly, I say to you, I am the door of the sheep.'"

John 13:5-8 "Then He poured water into a basin and began to wash the disciples' feet, and to wipe them with the towel with which He was girded. And so He came to Simon Peter, and Peter said to Him, 'Lord, do You wash my feet?' Jesus answered and said to him, 'What I do you do not realize now, but you shall understand hereafter.' Peter said to Him, 'Never shall You wash my feet!' Jesus answered him, 'If I do not wash you, you have no part with Me.'"

Jesus is the door and the doorkeeper and the One who knocks at the door of our heart. (Rev 3:20).

Day 239 Hos 2-4; Heb 13-James 1; Ps 85-87; Pr 10

James 1:22-25 "But prove yourselves doers of the word, and not merely hearers who delude themselves. For if anyone is a hearer of the word and not a doer, he is like a man who looks at his natural face in a mirror; for once he has looked at himself, and gone away; he has immediately forgotten what kind of person he was. But he who looks intently at the perfect law, the law of liberty and abides by it, not having become a forgetful hearer but an effectual doer, this man shall be blessed in what he does."

The mirror we look into is the Law, that moral code laid down through Moses. The law cannot purify us but shows us our weaknesses. For us, we cling to the mercy and grace Jesus paid for, but forgiveness is not an excuse to purposefully sin.

Mt 5:17-18 "Do not think that I came to abolish the Law or the Prophets; I did not come to abolish but to fulfill. For truly, I say to you, until heaven and earth pass away, not the smallest letter or stroke shall pass away from the Law until all is accomplished."

Day 240 Hos 5-7; James 2-3; Ps 88-90; Pr 11

James 3:2-5 & 8 "For we all stumble in many ways. If anyone does not stumble in what he says, he is a perfect man, able also to bridle the whole body as well. Now if we put the bits into the horses' mouths so that they may obey us, we direct their entire body as well. Behold, the ships also though they are so great and are driven by strong winds, are still directed by a very small rudder, wherever the inclination of the pilot desires. But no one can tame the tongue; it is a restless evil and full of deadly poison."

There is a recent study that tells that women use about 20,000 words per day and men 7,000. We talk all day long and how many of those words bring glory to our God? Probably not one out of ten words are useful let alone glorify our God.

Pr 10:19 "When there are many words, transgression is unavoidable, but he who restrains his lips is wise."

Day 241 Hos 8-10; James 4-5; Ps 91-93; Pr 12

Hos 9:1 "Do not rejoice, O Israel, with exaltation like nations! For you have played the harlot forsaking your God. You have loved harlots' earnings on every threshing floor.

Hos 10:12-13 "Sow with a view to righteousness, reap in accordance with kindness; break up your fallow ground, for it is time to seek the Lord, until He comes and rains righteousness on you. You have plowed wickedness; you have reaped injustice, you have eaten the fruit of lies, because you trusted in your way, in your numerous warriors,"

Again and again the love of the Lord reaches out to a people that are willfully blind. He calls them, He chastises them, He punishes them. Like a willful heifer that goes every way but into the stall where she will be fed and brushed and cleaned and cared for, till all her needs are met.

The word, chasten means: 1. To discipline by punishment or affliction. 2. To moderate; soften; temper. 3. To refine, purify.

Job 5:17-18 "Behold, how happy is the man whom God reproves; so do not despise the discipline of the Almighty. For He inflicts pain, and gives relief; He wounds, and His hands also heal."

Day 242 Hos 11-13; I Pet 1-2; Ps 94-96; Pr 13

Hosea 11:3-5 & 8 "Yet it is I who taught Ephraim to walk, I took them in My arms; but they did not know that I healed them. I led them with cords of a man, with bonds of love, and I became to them as one who lifts the yoke from their jaws; and I bent down and fed them. How can I give you up, O Ephraim? How can I surrender you, O Israel....My heart is turned over"

The Lord cries for rebellious Ephraim. He delays judgment and pleads for them to come back. Hosea also is heartbroken over them. Hosea was told to take a harlot for his wife (Hos 1:2) and be a sign for Israel but they ignored him too. He was a weeping prophet like Jeremiah to a people who would not repent.

Day 243 Hos 14-Joel 2; I Pet 3-4; Ps 97-99; Pr 14

I Pet 3:18 "For Christ also died for sins once for all, the just for the unjust, in order that He might bring us to God, having been put to death in the flesh, but made alive in the spirit;"

Col 2:13-14 "And when you were dead in your transgressions and the uncircumcision of your flesh, He made you alive together with Him, having forgiven us all our transgressions, having canceled out the certificate of debt consisting of decrees against us and which was hostile to us; and He has taken it out of the way, having nailed it to the cross."

We were dead, and have now been touched by the resurrection power, and the old life of self-seeking is gone. Everything we are now belongs to the Lord. And if we suffer for the Lord, we are so blessed.

Resistance builds strength, persecution builds fervor, so what kind of people do we chose to be?

Heb 12:3-4 "For consider Him who endured such hostility from sinners against Himself, so that you may not grow weary and lose heart. You have not yet resisted to the point of shedding blood in your striving against sin."

Day 244 Joel 3-Amos 2; I Pet 5-II Pet 1; Ps 100-102; Pr 15

Having our sins forgiven is a great thing but through the Holy Spirit we have so much more.

II Peter 1:3-4 "as His divine power has given to us all things that pertain to life and godliness, through the knowledge of Him who called us by glory and virtue, by which have been given to us exceedingly great and precious promises, that through these you may be partakers of the divine nature, having escaped the corruption that is in the world through lust."

We now have the divine nature! That nature carries us from faith to virtue, to knowledge, to self-control, to perseverance, to godliness, to brotherly kindness, coming at last to brotherly love. Love is the highest calling and is the essence of God the Father and Jesus.

Day 245 Amos 3-5; II Pet 2-3; Ps 103-105; Pr 16

Amos 3:3 "Can two walk together, unless they be agreed?" If you are a believer, do not marry an unbeliever.

II Cor 6:14-15 "Do not be bound together with unbelievers; for what partnership have righteousness and lawlessness, or what fellowship has light with darkness? Or what harmony has Christ with Belial, or what has a believer in common with an unbeliever? Or what agreement has the temple of God with idols? For you are the temple of the living God."

I Cor 7:10-15 "But to the married I give instructions, not I, but the Lord, that the wife should not leave her husband (but if she does leave, let her remain unmarried, or else be reconciled to her husband), and that the husband should not send his wife away. But to the rest I say not the Lord, that if any brother has a wife who is an unbeliever and she consents to live with him, let him not send her away. For the unbelieving husband is sanctified through his wife, and the unbelieving wife is sanctified through her believing husband; for otherwise your children are unclean, but now they are holy. Yet if the unbelieving one leaves, let him leave; the brother or the sister is not under bondage in such cases, but God has called us to peace.

Day 246 Amos 6-8; I John 1-2; Ps 106-108; Pr 17

Amos 8:2-3 "...The end has come for My people Israel; I will spare them no longer. And the songs of the palace will turn to wailing in that day,' declares the Lord God—'Many will be the corpses; in every place they will cast them forth in silence."

There were 8 Kings of Judah who "did what was right in the sight of the Lord." They didn't do everything right but at least made the attempt.

Kings 15:11-14 "And Asa did what was right in the sight of the Lord, like David his father. He also put away the male cult prostitutes from the land, and removed all the idols which his fathers had made.

And he also removed Maacah his mother from being queen mother, because she had made a horrid image as an Asherah; and Asa cut down her horrid image and burned it at the brook Kidron.

But the high places were not taken away; nevertheless the heart of Asa was wholly devoted to the Lord all his days."

The high places were a snare to the people of Judah over and over. From the dividing of the kingdom after Solomon, Israel had kings that did evil and led their people into idol worship.

Israel had one bad king after another, not one followed the Lord, His patience is long but finally Israel was carried away.

Amos 9:9 "For surely I will ...sift the house of Israel among all nations.

Day 247 Amos 9-Jonah 1; I John 3-4; Ps 109-111; Pr 18

Obadiah gave prophecy against Edom, the descendants of Esau. When Jacob returned from working for his wives and livestock, his brother Esau met him with joy. When Esau saw that the land was not enough to support both of them he moved his family to Mount Seir (Day 72). But Esau's descendants were always hostile to Jacob's descendants.

Obadiah 1:10-14 & 18 "Because of violence to your brother Jacob, you will be covered with shame, and you will be cut off forever. On the day that you stood aloof, on the day that strangers carried off his wealth, and foreigners entered his gate and cast lots for Jerusalem--- you too were as one of them. Do not gloat over your brother's day, the day of his misfortune. And do not rejoice over the sons of Judah in the day of their destruction; yes, do not boast in the day of their distress. Do not enter the gate of My people in the day of their disaster. Yes, you, do not gloat over their calamity in the day of their disaster, and do not loot their wealth in the day of their disaster. And do not stand at the fork of the road to cut down their fugitives; and do not imprison their survivors in the day of their distress. Then the house of Jacob will be a fire and the house of Joseph a flame; but the house of Esau will be as stubble. And they will set them on fire and consume them, so that there will be no survivor of the house of Esau,' for the Lord has spoken."

Day 248 Jonah 2-4; I John 5-II John 1; Ps 112-114; Pr 19

Jonah 1-4 Jonah was told to go to Nineveh but ran the other way. He was so prejudiced against the people of Nineveh that he would rather die than to preach to them. Here is a man who heard the voice of God and feared Him. Yet, he disobeyed because he knew God was merciful.

Jonah wanted all the people in that great city to be destroyed. When Nineveh repented from the king to the least of them, God had mercy on them and this made Jonah more angry than everything else.

Jesus was passing through Samaria and asked a woman there for a drink.

John 4:9 "The Samaritan woman therefore said to Him, 'How is it that You, being a Jew, ask me for a drink since I am a Samaritan woman?' (For Jews have no dealings with Samaritans.)"

The Jews knew that they were God's particular people but they did not share His love and compassion.

For the Church the primary command is love, love the Lord and love your neighbor and love your enemy even if they are from a despised group.

Day 249 Micah 1-3; III John-Jude; Ps 115-117; Pr 20

Jude 1:4 & 7 & 10 "For certain persons have crept in unnoticed, those who were long beforehand marked out for this condemnation, ungodly persons who turn the grace of our God into licentiousness and deny our only Master and Lord, Jesus Christ. Just as Sodom and Gomorrah and the cities around them, since they in the same way as these indulged in gross immorality and went after strange flesh, are exhibited as an example, in undergoing the punishment of eternal fire. But these men revile the things which they do not understand; and the things which they know by instinct, like unreasoning animals, by these things they are destroyed."

There were some who wanted the non-Jewish believers to be circumcised and follow all the rules and regulations of the Law. This group took the opposite view, that grace covered all sins, past and future so the Law was voided and you could follow any lust freely. Since the Law was always for our protection, it still holds true.

Day 250 Micah 4-6; Rev 1-2; Ps 118-120; Pr 21

Rev 1:5 "and from Jesus Christ, the faithful witness, the firstborn of the dead, and the ruler of the kings of the earth. …"

John 11:25 "Jesus said to her, I am the resurrection and the life, He who believes in Me, shall live even if he dies, and everyone who lives and believes in Me shall never die, …."

Before Jesus was resurrected the saints of old slept.

Daniel 12:2 "And many of those who sleep in the dust of the ground will awake, these to everlasting life, but the others to disgrace and everlasting contempt."

I K 2:10 "So David slept with his fathers, and was buried in the city of David." (KJV)

Deut 31:16 "And the Lord said to Moses: 'Behold, Thou will sleep with thy fathers; …. "(KJV)

But when Jesus hung on the cross, (Luke 23:43) He had the authority to tell the thief beside Him that they would be together in paradise that day.

Day 251 Micah 7-Nah 2; Rev 3-4; Ps 121-123; Pr 22

Ps 121:2-3 "My help comes from the Lord, who made heaven and earth. He will not allow your foot to slip; He who keeps you will not slumber."

John 10:29 "My Father, who has given them to Me, is greater than all; and no one is able to snatch them out of the Father's hand."

These verses are very reassuring and somewhat similar. But I think this means no person can take you away from the Lord. But, you still have a free will and you can move yourself away from the Lord, otherwise how can you fall away and come back with repentance, which Israel did constantly, (and is our example). If you make a conscious choice to sin, that places a barrier between you and the Lord and being unfruitful can remove you from Jesus (John 15). We should not be overly anxious if a bad word slips out, because we are surrounded with profanity everywhere, but do the best we can and pray about the rest. The Lord does not want to lose us and willingly forgives, but we must not be lax in trying to do right.

Day 252 Nah 3-Hab 2; Rev 5-6; Ps 124-126; Pr 23

David was a man who understood worship. Praise and worship are often spoken of as if they are the same. The Hebrew language is very rich with multiple meanings. From Strong's Exhaustive Concordance you can find the root meanings: (edited to prevent too much repetition)

Praise

3034---to hold out the hand, to throw,--to revere or worship with extended hands. To bemoan (by wringing the hands)--cast out, confess, make confession, give thanks
1974---in the sense of rejoicing; a celebration of thanksgiving for the harvest, merry.
1984---Prim root; to be clear (orig. of sound but usually of color); to shine; hence to make a show to shine.
8416---laudation, specifically a hymn: praise
1288---to kneel down; to bless God (as an act of adoration)
2167---(perhaps identified with 2168 to trim a vine, prune) through the idea of striking with the fingers: to touch the strings or parts of a musical instrument, play upon it; to make music with singing. Sing forth praises, psalms.
8426---Extend hand, make avowal
7612---to address in a loud tone--commend, glory, keep in praise, triumph,--to adulate, i.e. adore; shout His fame.

Worship;

7812---depress, i.e. prostrate. To do homage to royalty, to God: to bow down, crouch, fall down flat; humbly beseech, make obeisance, do reverence, make to stoop, worship.
4352---Pining, to be made thin i.e. be impoverished.

The best praise I've ever had was in a group and the best worship was when I was alone, face down on a bath towel on the floor weeping, and all I could say was thank You Father, thank You, thank You....

Day 253 Hab 3-Zeph 2; Rev 7-8; Ps 127-129; Pr 24

Rev 7:4-8 This is an odd list of the twelve sons of Jacob. First, they are not in the correct birth order, and Manasseh was grandson through Joseph. Joseph is listed later so who is left out and why? The meaning of the name is significant. These definitions are from the Strong's Concordance, my interpretation is in parentheses.

Judah: 3034 to throw out the hand; to revere or worship (with extended hands) to bemoan by wringing the hands. Cast out, make confession, praise, give thanks. (repent)

Reuben: 7205 See a son, (become saved)

Gad: 1410 from 1464 to crowd upon, i.e. attack: invade, overcome (from 1413; to crowd; also to gash as if pressing into):..assemble (selves by troops) gather selves together. (come into fellowship and warfare)

Asher: 836 from 833 to be straight, esp. to be level, right, happy; fig. to go forward, be honest, prosper. bless, guide, lead, relieve. (grow in faith, becoming more like Jesus)

Naphtali: 5321 from 6617 my wrestling. To twine. I.e. to struggle or to be (morally) tortuous. (deep prayer, intercession)

Manasseh: 4519 causing to forget; from 5388 –forgetfulness; oblivion, forget, remove. (able to give total forgiveness)

Simeon: 8095 to hear intelligently. (give attention and obey)

Levi: 3878 attached, from 8867 to twine, to unite, to remain, abide with, cleave, join (married, as the bride)

Issachar: 3485 he will bring a reward. (serving God by serving others)

Zebulun: 2074 habitation; from 2082 to enclose, to reside:--dwell with (always with Him)

Joseph: 3130 let him add; augment (evangelize)

Benjamin: 1144 Son of the right hand; son of my strength (mature at last)

These names show the path of a believer. We reach out to God and gain strength as we grow.

Dan, the son not on the list, is a characteristic that must not belong to us.

Dan: 1835 from 1777 to rule; to judge, contend, execute judgment, the judgment of God

Day 254 Zeph 3-Hag 2; Rev 9-10; Ps 130-132; Pr 25

Haggai had come back to Jerusalem from the Babylonian captivity and the people had to rebuild houses again, but twelve years had passed. Haggai was the first known prophet after the return from Babylon and The Lord called him to get the Temple rebuilt.

Haggai 1:7-10 & 14 "Thus says the Lord of hosts, 'Consider your ways! Go up to the mountains; bring wood and rebuild the temple, that I may be pleased with it and be glorified,' says the Lord. 'You look for much but behold it comes to little; when you bring it home, I blow it away. Why?' declares Lord of hosts. 'Because of My house which lies desolate, while each of you runs to his own house. Therefore, because of you the sky has withheld its dew, and the earth has withheld its produce. So the Lord stirred up the spirit of Zerubbabel the son of Shealtiel, governor of Judah, and the spirit of Joshua the son of Jehozadak, the high priest, and the spirit of all the remnant of the people, and they came and worked on the house of the Lord of hosts, their God,"

Malachi 3:10 "Bring the whole tithe into the storehouse, that there may be food in My house, and test Me now in this' says the Lord of hosts, 'If I will not open for you the windows of heaven and pour out for you such blessing until it overflows."

Leviticus 27:30 "Thus all the tithe of the land, of the seed of the land or of the fruit of the tree, is the Lord's, it is holy to the Lord."

Day 255 Zech 1-3; Rev 11-12; Ps 133-135; Pr 26

Heb 12:1 "Therefore, since we have so great a cloud of witnesses surrounding us, let us also lay aside every encumbrance, and the sin which so easily entangles us, ..."

What is the sin that so easily ensnares us?

Pr 26:11 "Like a dog that returns to its vomit is a fool who repeats his folly."

Habits are hard to change, if it was easy it would not be a habit. The devil is clever enough to separate us even in our main weakness. If you and I had the same flaw we could sympathize with and support each other. As it is we commit one of the worse sins, judging each other; I think my sin is understandable but yours is just ridiculous, etc. We have to come together.

James 5:16 "Therefore, confess your sins to one another, and pray for one another, so that you may be healed. The effective prayer of a righteous man can accomplish much."

Day 256 Zech 4-6; Rev 13-14; Ps 136-138; Pr 27

Zech 6:12-13 & 15 "Then say to him, 'Thus says the Lord of hosts, "Behold a man whose name is Branch, for He will branch out from where He is; and He will build the temple of the Lord. Yes, it is He who will build the temple of the Lord, and He who will bear the honor and sit and rule on His throne.

Thus, He will be a priest on His throne, and the counsel of peace will be between the two offices." "And those who are far off will come and build the temple of the Lord' Then you will know that the Lord of hosts has sent me to you. And it will take place, if you completely obey the Lord your God."

This is how godly people of the Old Testament were saved through faith in Jesus, the Christ, who had not yet bought their forgiveness with His blood. Promises made to them starting with Eve and being repeated again and again through His prophets and servants. Their faith was laid on a foundation of the promises of a God who had never lied to them. Our faith is built on the same promises, but on His completed sacrifice.

Day 257 Zech 7-9; Rev 15-16; Ps 139-141; Pr 28

Rev 16:1-2 "Then I heard a loud voice from the temple saying to the seven angels, 'Go and pour out the seven bowls of the wrath of God on the earth. And the first angel went and poured out his bowl into the earth, and it became a loathsome and malignant sore upon the men who had the mark of the beast and who worshiped his image."

Ez 9:1-6 "Then he cried out in my hearing with a loud voice saying, 'Draw near, O executioners of the city each with his destroying weapon in his hand. And behold, six men came from the direction of the upper gate which faces north, each with his shattering weapon in his hand; and among them was a certain man clothed in linen with a writing case at his loins. And they went in and stood beside the bronze altar. Then the glory of the God of Israel went up from the cherub on which it had been, to the threshold of the temple. And He called to the man clothed in linen at whose loins was the writing case.

And the Lord said to him, 'Go through the midst of the city, even through the midst of Jerusalem, and put a mark on the foreheads of the men who sigh and groan over all the abominations which are being committed in its midst.' But to the others He said in my hearing, 'Go through the city after him and strike; do not let your eye have pity, and do not spare. Utterly slay old men, young men, maidens, little children, and women, but do not touch any man on whom is the mark; and you shall start from My sanctuary.' So they started with the elders who were before the temple."

You may not see the mark of God but if you belong to Jesus, you have it already.

Day 258 Zech 10-12; Rev 17-18; Ps 142-144; Pr 29

Zech 11:4 & 7-8 "Thus says the Lord my God: Shepherd the flock destined for slaughter, so I (Zechariah) shepherded the flock of slaughter, truly (as the name implies) the most miserable of sheep. And I took two shepherd's staffs, the one I called Beauty or Grace, and the other I called Bands or Union; and I fed and shepherded the flock. And I cut off the three shepherds (the civil authorities, the priests and the prophets) in one month, for I was weary and impatient with them, and they also loathed me."(Amplified)

The Prophets were usually feared and hated. They were always crying out against the sin and idol worship. While we can see their weakness and even get tired of these people who wobbled between two choices, and most often chose the wrong one, they were at a big disadvantage to us, for we have the indwelling Holy Spirit, He is always with us.

Day 259 Zech 13-Mal 1; Rev 19-20; Ps 145-147; Pr 30

Rev 20:4 "And I saw thrones, and they sat upon them, and judgment was given to them, and I saw the souls of those who had been beheaded because of the testimony of Jesus and because of the word of God, and those who had not worshiped the beast or his image, and had not received the mark upon their forehead and upon their hand; and they came to life and reigned with Christ for a thousand years.

Rev 7:14 "And I said to him, 'My lord, you know.' And he said to me, 'These are the ones who come out of the great tribulation, and they have washed their robes and made them white in the blood of the Lamb.'"

I was taught to believe in a pre-tribulation rapture which would take the Church away at the beginning of the seven years of the tribulation. But the Bible took that comfortable belief away from me. Is it only in the United States that the Church is so weak that we want to believe we shouldn't suffer for our faith? Christians are being killed every day for their faith, by communists in China and N. Korea and many died in the Russian purges. Muslims feel threatened by Christians and many believers this minute are being beaten, starved, tortured and killed in unspeakable ways. Why should we not suffer?

Day 260 Mal 2-4; Rev 21-22; Ps 148-150; Pr 31

Rev 22:18-19 "For I testify to everyone who hears the words of the prophecy of this book: If anyone adds to them, God will add to him the plagues which are written in this book; and if anyone takes away from the words of the book of this prophecy, God shall take away his part from the tree of life and from the holy city, which are written in this book."

II Tim 3:16-17 "All Scripture is inspired by God, and profitable for teaching, for reproof, for correction, for training in righteousness; that the man of God may be adequate, equipped for every good work."

Pr 6:23 "For the commandment is a lamp, and the law is light; and reproofs for discipline are the way of life,"

De 4:2 You shall not add to the word which I am commanding you; nor take away from it, that you may keep the commandments of the Lord your God which I command you."

There are divisions in the Church because of dividing the Word and making one part more or less important than the other. An entire denomination may be built on a single scripture. The Church has lost its strength because we are not a single unit.

Eccl 4:9-12 "Two are better than one, because they have a good return for their labor. For if either of them falls, the one will lift up his companion, But woe to the one who falls when there is not another to lift him up. Furthermore, if two lie down together they keep warm; but how can one be warm alone?

And if one can overpower him who is alone, two resist him. A cord of three strands is not quickly torn apart."

Mt 18:20 "For where two or three have gathered together in My name, there I am in their midst."

If you should choose to read the Bible through again, I hope you will take another translation; I particularly love the Amplified Bible.